CW01497387

1 MONTH OF
FREE
READING

at

www.ForgottenBooks.com

By purchasing this book you are eligible for one month membership to ForgottenBooks.com, giving you unlimited access to our entire collection of over 1,000,000 titles via our web site and mobile apps.

To claim your free month visit:
www.forgottenbooks.com/free1048405

* Offer is valid for 45 days from date of purchase. Terms and conditions apply.

ISBN 978-0-331-79994-1
PIBN 11048405

This book is a reproduction of an important historical work. Forgotten Books uses
state-of-the-art technology to digitally reconstruct the work, preserving the original format
whilst repairing imperfections present in the aged copy. In rare cases, an imperfection in
the original, such as a blemish or missing page, may be replicated in our edition. We do,
however, repair the vast majority of imperfections successfully; any imperfections that
remain are intentionally left to preserve the state of such historical works.

Forgotten Books is a registered trademark of FB &c Ltd.
Copyright © 2018 FB &c Ltd.
FB &c Ltd, Dalton House, 60 Windsor Avenue, London, SW19 2RR.
Company number 08720141. Registered in England and Wales.

For support please visit www.forgottenbooks.com

B 499341 E

616.85
O37
T65

FIFTEENTH ANNUAL REPORT

— OF THE —

Board of Trustees and Officers

— OF THE —

Toledo State Hospital

— TO THE —

GOVERNOR OF THE STATE OF OHIO,

— FOR THE —

Fiscal Year Ending November 15, 1898.

FIFTEENTH ANNUAL REPORT

— OF THE —

Board of Trustees and Officers

— OF THE —

Toledo State Hospital

— TO THE —

GOVERNOR OF THE STATE OF OHIO,

— FOR THE —

Fiscal Year Ending November 15, 1898.

COLUMBUS, OHIO.
The Westbote Co., State Printers.
1899.

BOARD OF TRUSTEES.

Charles Foster.. Fostoria.
Parks Foster .... Elyria.
G. P. Campbell, M. D.. Wauseon.
William Geyser .... Swanton.
L. C. Cole.. Bowling Green.

OFFICERS.

H. A. TOBEY, M. D.. Superintendent.
A. F. SHEPHERD, M. D... Assistant Physician.
W. G. COOPER, M. D... "
E. G. LUPTON, M. D... "
G. R. LOVE, M. D.. "
R. B. LEISTER, M. D.. "
C. S. MILLER .... Steward.
E. M. GARRETT... Storekeeper.
MRS. M. C. TOBEY.. Matron.

REPORT OF TRUSTEES.

HON. ASA S. BUSHNELL, Governor:

This hospital continues to retain its high standard of excellence in all respects, as well as in its economy of management. The operations for the current year have been uneventful, except in the distressing death of Dr. F. A. Todd, our senior assistant physician. Dr. Todd, while in the discharge of his duties, encountered a mad dog, and in his effort to prevent the animal from doing harm to patients, was himself bitten in the thumb. He went to the Pasteur Institute in Chicago for treatment, but without avail. He died within five weeks of hydrophobia, a most distressing death. The doctor was one of the ablest staff officers we have had, and we sincerely mourn his untimely taking off.

The cost of maintenance has been as follows: Total cost for current expenses and officers' salaries, $167,514.62; average number of patients resident during year, 1,400; per capita cost, $119.65.

Progress has been made toward increasing the comfort and amusements of our people.

On August 29 we were visited by the first fire of any moment in our history, which consumed our morgue and storage sheds, the money cost of the loss being about $5,000. Through the kindness of the Emergency Board, a handsome brick morgue and also an ample storage shed of brick have taken the place of the wooden structures destroyed by the fire.

Contracts were let for additions to three cottages at a cost of $6,075, which only included the construction of the new portions. The remainder of the work of remodeling these cottages and two others, has been done by persons we employed by the day, under the direction of the superintendent. Two of the cottages that have been remodeled are occupied, and the work on the other three is approaching completion. A contract was also let for the construction of a hospital building for male patients, provided for by the last appropriation act of the General Assembly, which will be completed and occupied by the 1st of next June. The additions to cottages, with the new hospital, will increase our capacity to fully 1,500 patients. The appropriations for sewage tank, engine and pumps for the completion of the sewage disposal works, have been and will be expended in time to secure a test of its utility as a fertilizer, which we are looking forward to in the expectation of realizing all we have hoped for. We have already demonstrated with the sewage beds we have in use the entire practicability of sewage disposal.

It is again a great pleasure to us to testify to the faithfulness of the staff, the steward, the matron, the storekeeper, the supervisors, the attendants, and all of the employes, with whose loyalty, fidelity and capacity our success is due. They all have the sincere thanks of the Board.

CHARLES FOSTER, *President,*
PARKS FOSTER, *Vice-President,*
G. P. CAMPBELL, *M. D.,*
WILLIAM GEYSER,
L. C. COLE,
Trustees.

SUPERINTENDENT'S REPORT.

To the Honorable Board of Trustees of the Toledo State Hospital:

GENTLEMEN: The end of another fiscal year renders it incumbent upon me to present for your consideration the superintendent's report of the operations of the institution under your control, this being the fifteenth annual report. By refering to table No. 1 it will be seen that there were 1,405 patients remaining at the end of last year. 732 men and 673 women. There have been admitted during the year, 372 patients, 207 men and 165 women, making the total number under treatment 1,777, 939 men and 838 women, of which number there were discharged recovered, 104, 63 men and 41 women, improved, 54, 26 men and 28 women, unimproved, 22, 14 men and 8 women, not insane 3, 2 men and 1 woman, died 82, 45 men and 37 women, and on September the 5th, 73 men and 53 women, making a total of 126 persons, were transferred to the Massillon State Hospital, and on the order of the Governor, 1 male patient was transferred to the Dayton State Hospital, making the total number removed from the hospital 392, 224 men and 168 women, leaving at the date of this report 1,385 patients, 715 of whom are men and 670 are women. The average number resident during the year was 1,400, 730 men, 670 women.

The percentage of recoveries, based on the total number admitted was 27.96 per cent., and the percentage of deaths based on the whole number under treatment was 4.61 per cent.

The per capita cost, based upon the funds drawn from the State Treasury, including current expenses and officers' salaries, was $119.65. Based upon the same and including receipts from all sources, was $129.19.

The percentage of recoveries is about the same as that of last year, but it is higher than the average rate of recoveries for former years, which is due, as stated in the last annual report, to the fact that the institution has been so overcrowded that it has been necessary to restrict admissions to the more acute and favorable cases.

The percentage of deaths is lower than ever before, which is in part due to the same cause that has increased the recovery rate. The improvements that have been made in the sanitary conditions of the buildings for patients from year to year, no doubt has contributed much to this favorable result.

It is gratifying to be able to report that the institution has been entirely free from any diseases, epidemic or contagious in character, except a few cases of erysipelas. By reference to the table showing causes of death, it will be seen that but one person has died of acute physical disease. There have been two suicides, both by drowning, and one death resulting from burns received while a patient was being bathed. While occurrences of this kind are always distressing and painful, and can usually be attributed to a lack of judgment or carelessness on the part of some one, yet it is surprising that with so large a number of insane persons cared for, the number of casualities are so few.

The year just closed is one of the most successful in the history of the institution, as is shown by the high rate of recovery, the low rate of mortality, and a lower than the average rate of maintainance, notwithstanding the advance in prices of many staple articles over former years.

The affairs of the institution have run smoothly and harmoniously, and we have been free from strife or contention, and the officers and employes, almost without exception, have manifested a commendable zeal and earnestness in the performance of their several duties.

As in former years, every privilege, liberty or pleasure has been accorded to patients that has been deemed consistent with their respective conditions, and every means at our command has been put forth to furnish useful and healthful occupation. Nor have we relaxed in our efforts to provide amusements and entertainments. Probably as often as twice a week for the entire year, our patients have been assembled on the campus or in the amusement hall for amusements and entertainments. On two occasions upwards of 400 went to the city to witness the street parades of circuses. As large a number attended the tri-State Fair and upwards of 700 took a day's outing at the Casino, a resort some 12 miles from the institution. There was not an instance of unbecoming behavior or escape, or an attempt at escape, on any of these excursions. Last winter during the sleighing season parties of patients were taken out every day that the weather would permit, for sleigh rides. A carry-all was purchased last summer, and during the pleasant weather has been used almost daily for taking patients riding.

The Legislature at their last session gave us larger appropriations for improvements and betterments than the institution has ever received since it was organized, consequently the past season has been one of great activity in this line. Five cottages have been completely remodeled, overhauled, and additions built to four of them, increasing their capacity for about 38 patients. The remodeling of these cottages has been thoroughly done. From two to three large chimneys for ventilation have been built for each one, the floors both upstairs and down have been renewed, the ceilings replastered, they have been provided with new and thorough sanitary plumbing, and in two of them, basement rooms have been converted into clothing rooms and bath rooms, giving the rooms on the first floor formerly occupied for this purpose, for other uses. Two of the cottages at this date are completed, except the interior decorations, and are occupied. Two others are almost finished and the work on the other is well under way. In the early part of the season, by using the chapel for a cottage and greatly overcrowding the wards and cottages, we were enabled to vacate two cottages at a time, which were put in order as rapidly as possible. After the removal of 126 patients to the Massillon State Hospital and re-occupying the cottages that had been vacated, we were enabled to vacate three other cottages, two of which, as before stated, are approaching completion. An addition has been built for the kitchen, 35 by 40 feet, occupying the space between the bakery and the covered way, which is used as a scullery, and a room for preparing food for the kitchen. A bake oven has been built in connection with the kitchen and two cold storage rooms have been added. The room that was used for a scullery has been converted into a room for storing flour and two small rooms, one for each the bakery and kitchen, for general stores. Each of the general dining rooms has been provided with a dish washer and a line of shafting run from the dining rooms to the kitchen, where an engine has been put in for furnishing power for the dish washers, for driving a fan in the kitchen, running a coffee grinder, meat chopper, ice cream freezer, and a three-barrel bread mixer that has been installed in the bakery. A space 30 by 75 feet has been paved with paving brick laid in cement, back of the kitchen, forming a court for the garbage wagon. A small addition has been built to the building used for shops and a 25 horse-power automatic Russell engine has been installed. A pipe cutting and threading machine that will cut up to a six-inch pipe has been added to our machine shop and a power mortising machine added to the carpenter shop. A water heater, which automatically controls the temperature of the water, has been placed in the basement of each of the buildings for disturbed patients and a two-inch main has been carried entirely around through the duct, a distance of 2,600 feet, supplying every building with water for bath and lavaratory purposes. The temperature at which these heaters will deliver water is set below scalding point, and therefore the possibility of such accidents as reported both last year and this, is precluded. The electric mains in the duct from the boiler house to the duct for the front row of buildings, on account of the duct being so crowded with pipes, frequently became grounded and we were constantly in danger of burning out the dynamos and leaving the institution in darkness, therefore a duct four by five feet, 300 feet in length, was constructed and the mains placed in it, supported on glass insulators. One thousand feet of eight-inch cast iron pipe was laid from the lakes to connect with the pumps at the boiler house, provided with suitable valves and connections to increase the supply of water to the pumps, as the six-inch main, with the increased demand for water, had become insufficient. Eight hundred feet of two-inch steam pipe was run in the duct from the boiler house to one of the buildings for disturbed patients to supply one of the water heaters spoken of. Nine thousand feet of steam pipe has been covered with non-conducting covering. A new feed water pump has been placed in the boiler house and a large amount of work done in repairs in the engineer's department. Two acres of sewage beds have been prepared, and the dike along the creek a distance of 1,500 feet has been raised 18 inches, we having found by last spring's freshets that the beds were liable to be overflowed. A tank for sewage, 40 feet in diameter and eight feet deep, with a capacity of 60,000 gallons, is just approaching completion. During the greater portion of the summer we had but about six acres of sewage beds that were available, but with this area we were able to satisfactorily take care of our sewage, although the beds were constantly overtaxed. There was but little odor about the beds and the effluent coming from them was perfectly clear and odorless. With the use of the additional beds that were added this season it is believed that the problem of sewage disposal for the institution has been satisfactorily solved. A cement walk 475 feet in length and seven feet wide has been made from the entrance to the grounds to the administration building, which supplies a long felt want and is a comfort to all persons going to and from the institution. A greenhouse, 150 feet long by 25 feet wide, of substantial construction, is just being completed for growing winter vegetables and propogating plants for the garden. During the summer and fall all the slate roofs and all the gutters and down spouts have been repaired and largely renewed, and have been repainted. This work has required a force of two tinners with a helper, and three painters. On the 20th of August the storage sheds and a small frame building used for a morgue, were destroyed by fire. The fire was discovered about nine o'clock in the evening and originated from spontaneous combustion in a pile of rags that were in the shed. As the sheds were filled with combustible materials the fire spread rapidly and could not be controlled until the sheds, with the building spoken of, were practically destroyed, and it was with difficulty that we kept the fire from extending to other buildings. The Emergency Board authorized us to make a deficiency of $5,000 in the ordinary repair fund, with which to build a morgue and rebuild the sheds, and a contract for the work was let on September 24. The morgue will be of brick and there will be four rooms on the first floor, one of which will be used as a chapel, and one as a receiving room for dead bodies, where they can be dressed and prepared, in connection with which there will be a cold storage room, and two other rooms on the first floor and a room on the second floor will be used for pathological laboratories. A new hospital building for men is being erected in the space between the extreme cottage on the front row and the building for disturbed male patients. This will be the most ornamental building on the grounds and will accommodate 75 patients and has three complete wards or departments. This building, with the enlargements that have been made to cottages this season, and the additions that will be built to cottages next year, will give the institution an increased capacity for 130 patients, bringing the total capacity up to about 1,500.

On February 17, Mr. R. E. Hamblin resigned the position of steward and was succeeded by Mr. C. S. Miller, who for four years had been the storekeeper. The position of storekeeper, made vacant by the promotion of Mr. Miller, was filled by the appointment of Mr. Ephraim M. Garrett. Dr. Fred A. Todd, my first assistant, died at the Presbyterian Hospital in Chicago, of hydrophobia, on September the 30th. On August 29, just as the doctor had started out to make his morning visits to the cottages, he met a strange dog of good size, to which he reached out his hand and snapped his finger. As he did so the dog sprang at him and caught him by the end of the thumb of the right hand, tearing off the nail and lacerating the thumb. The wound was immediately cauterized and dressed. The dog was killed a few minutes later. A post mortem examination, made by a Veterinary Surgeon, Dr. J. V. Newton, showed the dog's stomach to be filled with pebbles, sticks and straw, but no food, and the glands about the neck to be enlarged and congested. The carcass was sent to Dr. O. P. Ohlmacher, the Pathologist and Bacteriologist of the State Hospital for Epileptics at Gallipolis. Three rabbits were inoculated, all of which were taken, in from 18 to 20 days with rabies, and died. After a dog that had been bitten by the dog that bit Dr. Todd developed hydrophobia, and one of the rabbits that had been inoculated showed unmistakable symptoms of the disease, the doctor was persuaded to go to Chicago and take the Pasteur treatment, although he thought it was useless to do so, because his wound had healed so kindly, and had been so promptly and well cared for. After being in Chicago two weeks he developed hydrophobia and was taken to the Presbyterian Hospital, where after four days of terrible anguish, he died. Dr. Todd was a man of strong personal characteristics; he was brave, honorable and kind; he was warm and true in his friendships, was frank and outspoken, and never resorted to deception or subtefuges. He was systematic, faithful and painstaking in the discharge of his duties, even to the smallest, and considered no duty a hardship that contributed to the welfare of his patients, or to the benefit of the institution. In his death the institution has lost a valuable officer, the patients a kind and capable physician, and his colleagues a delightful companion and true friend.

On October 17, Dr. George R. Lowe was elected to the position of assistant physician, made vacant by the death of Dr. Todd, and Dr. R. B. Leister was also elected assistant physician at this meeting, as an additional officer. At the date of the last annual report there was a vacancy on the staff for an assistant physician, which was filled on December 17, by the election of Dr. Ella G. Lupton to the position.

Dr. A. F. Shepherd and Dr. W. G. Cooper continue to perform their duties in the same intelligent, zealous manner that has always characterized them. To them, and to all the officers that compose the staff, I desire to express my gratitude and appreciation for their many acts of personal kindness, and for the faithful manner in which they have discharged their respective duties. Our thanks are due to Rev. A. J. Jennings, who as often as every two weeks, has conducted religious services, and to a number of other clergymen who from time to time have officiated. We are also indebted to Rev.

David H. Moore, editor of the Christian Advocate, for a very delightful and eloquent address on the Fourth of July, also to Gen. Brinkerhoff, President State Board of Charities, and to Rev. J. Wesley Hill, who made very appropriate remarks on that occasion. In this connection I wish to express my gratitude to Mr. Sol Smith Russell, who gave us a very delightful entertainment, and will be gratefully remembered for a long time by many of our patients. Our thanks are also due to the large number of publishers of newspapers and periodicals, who contribute their papers to the institution, and to a number of news stands and persons who furnish us with periodicals and reading matter.

Another year, gentlemen of the Board, places me under renewed obligations to you for the firm support, wise counsel, and friendly aid that you have at all times extended to me. Hoping that I may be able to merit your continued confidence and that the coming year may be as successful as the one just past, I remain,

Respectfully,

H. A. TOBEY,
Superintendent.

TABLE I.

SHOWING ADMISSIONS, REMOVALS AND DEATHS FOR YEAR ENDING NOV. 15, 1898.

				M.	W.	T.
Remaining November 15, 1897..				732	673	1,405
	M.	W.	T.			
Admitted—						
First admissions..	177	180	307			
Re-admissions.....................	30	35	65			
Total number admitted......				207	165	372
Total number under care during year..				939	838	1,777
	M.	W.	T.			
Discharged—						
Recovered	63	41	104			
Improved......	26	28	54			
Unimproved	14	8	22			
Not insane	2	1	3			
Died	45	37	82			
Transferred to Massillon	78	53	126			
" Dayton	1	....	1			
Total number removed				224	168	392
Remaining November 15, 1898				715	670	1,385
Average number resident during year......				730	670	1,400

Percentage of recoveries based on number admitted............................... 27.96
"   deaths based on whole number under treatment................. 4.61

TABLE II.

SMOWING RESULTS SINCE OPENING OF HOSPITAL.

	M.	W.	T.
Admissions—			
First admissions	2,288	2,018	4,306
Re-admissions	277	244	521
Total number admitted	2,565	2,262	4,827

	M.	W.	T.	M.	W.	T.
Discharged—						
Recovered	608	491	1,099			
Improved	320	878	698			
Unimproved	309	220	529			
Not insane	21	15	36			
Died	518	435	953			
Transferred to other hospitals	74	53	127			
Total number removed				1,850	1,592	3,442
Remaining November 15, 1898				715	670	1.385
Average number resident for eleven years				589	569	1,158

TABLE III.

SHOWING CAUSES OF DEATH DURING YEAR ENDING NOVEMBER 15, 1898, WITH AGE AT DEATH.

	Between 15 and 20.		Between 20 and 30.		Between 30 and 40.		Between 40 and 50.		Between 50 and 60.		Between 60 and 70.		Between 70 and 80.		Unknown.		Total.		
	M.	W.	M.	W.	M.	W.	M.	W.	M.	W.	M.	W.	M.	W.	M.	W.	M.	W.	T.
Apoplexy, cerebral									1			1					1		4
Asphyxia									1								1		1
Cirrhosis, hepatic				8					1								1		1
Dementia, terminal					2	2		1		1								8	8
Epilepsy							1	2									4	2	6
Erysipelas, facial							1										1		1
Gangrene, senile													1				1		1
Insanity, confusional									1								1		1
Insanity, paralytic					1								1				1		1
Mania, acute						8	1	2	1	2		2					2	9	11
Mania, chronic				1	2	1		2	2								2		5
Marasmus							4	2		1							4		8
Melancholia, acute							1	2									2		2
Melancholia, stuporous									3								1	4	8
Nephritis, chronic					1												3		2
Organic disease of heart					7		4		5		1						16		1
Paretic dementia							1						1					1	17
Senility													1				1		1
Shock from burn																	1		1
Suicide by drowning			1							1							1	1	2
Tuberculosis pulmonum				2		2		1										4	4
Totals			1	6	13	10	11	10	14	6	2	5	4				45	37	82

TABLE IV.

Showing Admissions, Discharges and Deaths, With Annual Mortality, Proportion of Recoveries, Those Remaining at the Close of Each Year, and Average Number Resident Each Year.

Year.	Admitted.			Discharged.									Died.			Remaining Nov. 15, each year.			Percentage of recoveries on admissions.			Percentage of deaths on whole number under treatment.			Average number resident.		
				Recovered.			Improved.			Unimproved.																	
	M.	W.	T.	M.	W.	T.	M.	W.	T.	M.	W.	T.	M.	W.	T.	M.	W.	T.	M.	W.	T.	M.	W.	T.	M.	W.	T.
1888	540	517	1,057	45	40	85	15	23	38	6	8	14	29	19	48	444	424	868	8.93	7.78	8.08	5.37	3.67	4.52	374	360	734
1889	252	258	510	71	50	121	30	25	55	10	18	28	39	38	77	544	553	1,097	28.17	19.38	28.77	5.60	5.57	5.58	492	484	976
1890	202	165	367	77	55	132	21	28	49	24	8	32	50	48	98	574	581	1,155	33.12	33.83	35.72	6.66	5.97	6.28	563	555	1,119
1891	166	148	314	77	67	144	15	44	59	15	5	20	43	35	78	586	576	1,164	43.68	45.27	45.86	5.79	4.80	5.30	583	577	1,160
1892	175	174	349	33	48	81	32	23	60	50	35	85	59	48	107	586	591	1,177	19.26	27.59	23.42	7.78	6.40	7.06	574	575	1,149
1893	196	155	341	42	38	80	34	33	67	52	41	98	53	38	91	587	595	1,182	22.52	24.51	28.51	7.12	5.22	6.17	591	583	1,174
1894	205	168	373	39	40	79	41	40	81	66	40	106	43	49	94	600	595	1,196	19.08	28.81	21.18	5.48	6.29	5.85	599	584	1,183
1895	207	160	367	45	35	80	32	36	68	44	28	72	50	41	91	634	614	1,248	21.78	21.37	21.80	6.20	5.43	5.83	614	601	1,215
1896	210	177	387	51	36	87	42	60	92	16	23	39	58	46	104	684	624	1,308	24.29	20.32	22.48	6.57	5.82	6.36	655	621	1,276
1897	215	175	390	65	41	106	26	60	75	12	11	23	47	41	88	782	673	1,405	23.33	23.43	27.18	5.23	5.18	5.18	707	644	1,351
1898	207	165	372	63	41	104	26	28	54	14	8	22	45	37	82	715	670	1,385	30.43	21.97	27.96	4.90	4.41	4.61	730	670	1,400
Totals	2,565	2,262	4,827	608	491	1,099	320	378	698	309	220	529	518	435	968												

TABLE V.

Showing Duration of Insanity in Those Admitted, Recovered and Died During the Year Ending November 15, 1898.

Duration of insanity.	Admitted.			Recovered.			Died.		
	M.	W.	T.	M.	W.	T.	M.	W.	T.
Under 1 month	47	48	95				3	3	6
From 1 to 3 months	44	38	82	5	6	11	2	11	13
" 3 to 6 "	34	23	57	15	11	26	4		4
" 6 to 9 "	15	9	24	13	6	19	2	1	3
" 9 to 12 "	1	3	4	8	4	12	1		1
" 1 to 2 years	26	13	39	7	9	16	8	3	11
" 2 to 3 "	18	13	31	7	4	11	6	5	11
" 3 to 5 "	9	9	18	3	1	4	7	1	8
" 5 to 7 "	4	1	5	1		1	3	3	6
" 7 to 9 "	2	1	3					5	5
" 9 to 11 "	1	3	4				1		1
" 11 to 13 "		1	1					1	1
" 13 to 15 "		2	2				2	1	3
" 15 to 20 "							1		1
" 20 to 25 "									
Over 25 years	1	1	2	4		4		2	2
Unknown	5		5				5	1	6
Totals	207	165	372	63	41	104	45	37	82

TABLE VI.

SHOWING AGES OF ADMITTED, RECOVERED, DIED AND REMAINING IN THE YEAR ENDING NOVEMBER 15, 1898.

Ages.	Admitted.			Recovered.			Died.			Remaining Nov. 15, 1898.		
	M.	W.	T.	M.	W.	T.	M.	W.	T.	M.	W.	T.
Under 15 years	7	6	13							3	6	9
From 15 to 20 years	20	6	26	2	3	5				33	20	53
" 20 to 25 "	25	18	43	4	6	10				77	50	127
" 25 to 30 "	31	21	52	8	6	14	1	5	6	65	55	120
" 30 to 35 "	32	32	64	7	5	12	3	4	7	99	96	195
" 35 to 40 "	20	27	47	11	7	18	10	7	17	116	95	211
" 40 to 45 "	19	12	31	7	4	11	5	8	13	86	90	176
" 45 to 50 "	26	24	50	12	4	16	6	2	8	136	133	269
" 50 to 60 "	19	17	36	7	5	12	12	6	18	62	80	142
" 60 to 70 "	3		3	4	1	5	3	5	8	16	15	31
" 70 to 75 "	2		2	1		1	3		3	5	9	14
" 75 to 80 "		1	1				2		2		2	2
" 80 to 85 "		1	1							2	2	4
Over 85 years												
Unknown	3		3							15	17	32
Totals	207	165	372	63	41	104	45	37	82	715	670	1,385

TABLE VII.

SHOWING CIVIL CONDITION OF PATIENTS ADMITTED, RECOVERED AND DIED DURING YEAR ENDING NOVEMBER 15, 1898.

	Admitted.			Recovered.			Died.		
	M.	W.	T.	M.	W.	T.	M.	W.	T.
Single	83	37	120	23	13	36	8	11	19
Married	104	104	208	34	27	61	29	20	49
Wid'd	16	28	39	2	1	3	4	5	9
Divorced	3	1	4	2	....	2	2	....	2
Unknown	1	....	1	2	....	2	2	1	3
Totals	207	165	372	63	41	104	45	37	82

TABLE VIII.

SHOWING ALLEGED CAUSES OF INSANITY OF PATIENTS ADMITTED DURING YEAR ENDING NOVEMBER 15, 1898.

Alleged causes.	Predisposing.			Exciting.		
	M.	W.	T.	M.	W.	T.
ate fer......						
Cardiac dilatation					1	1
Childbirth					8	8
Cigarette smoking	1		1		1	1
Cerebro spial meningitis					1	1
Cerebral apoplexy	2		2			
Chorea				1		
Domestic trouble	2	3	5	2	5	7
Debility					1	1
Disappointment in love					1	1
Epilepsy	3		3	2	1	3
Exposure	1		1			
Financial trouble		2	2		1	
Gastric uh						
Grief				10	9	19
Heredity	44	46	90	2	1	1
Head injury	9		9	2	10	12
Hemiplegia				1	1	2
Ill health	6	2	8	3	5	1
Inhalation of vitalized air					5	8
Intemperance	30		30	5	1	5
Insolation	9		9	2		2
Imprisonment				1		1
Kidney disease					1	2

TABLE VIII—Concluded.

Alleged causes.	Predisposing.			Exciting.		
	M.	W.	T.	M.	W.	T.
La grippe	2	1	3		1	1
Mental derangement		2	2	9	1	10
Masturbation	13		13		2	2
Malarial fever		2	2		5	5
Menopause	3		3			
Narcotics					2	2
Heredity						
Overwork	5		5	3	11	14
Pregnancy					2	2
Previous attacks	27	29	56			
Privation					2	2
Puberty	2		2			
Religious excitement	2		2	4	11	15
Syphilis	6		6		1	1
Senility	5		5		1	1
Sexual perversion	1		1			
Sexual excesses				2		2
Typhoid fever	3	1	4			
Traumatism					1	1
Uterine trouble					3	3
Worry	2	7	9	12	7	19

TABLE IX.

Showing form of mental disease in admissions, recoveries and deaths during year ending November 15, 1898, and of all those remaining in the hospital on that date.

Form of mental disease.	Admitted			Recovered			Died			Remaining Nov. 15, 1898.		
	M.	W.	T.	M.	W.	T.	M.	W.	T.	M.	W.	T.
Adolescent insanity	1		1	1		1						
Alcoholic "	12	1	13	7	2	9				7		7
Circular "							3		3	2		2
_____ "	5		5	1		1				6	2	8
Primary							1		1			
Senile		4	4							4	4	8
Terminal	3	3	6					13	13	70	261	331
Epilepsy— Acquired	1		1				3		3	18	4	22
Congenital	1		1				1		1	15		15
Imbecile	3	5	8							14	13	27
Kleptomania		1	1							2	1	3
Mania— Simple	16	13	29	5	6	11	1		1	22	17	39
Acute	28	31	59	15	12	27	2	11	13	18	22	40
Chronic	10	9	19				3	3	6	147	157	304
Epileptic	4	4	8							4	16	20
Periodic										19	12	31
Melancholia— Senile		4	4					1	1	2	4	6
Simple	24	36	60	12	9	21	9	5	14	41	17	58
Acute	43	37	80	19	11	30	1	3	4	39	36	75
Chronic	3	9	12							155	71	226

TABLE IX—Concluded.

Form of mental disease.	Admitted.			Recovered.			Died.			Remaining Nov. 15, 1898.		
	M.	W.	T.	M.	W.	T.	M.	W.	T.	M.	W.	T.
Mania	8		8							4		4
...ic insanity	3		3	3		3	1		1	4		4
Paranoia	15	2	17					1	1	83	24	107
Paretic dmentia	22	3	25				20	1	21	30	3	33
...nt sanity	3	1	4		1	1				1	3	4
Puerperal "		1	1									
Sexual pervert	2		2							7	3	10
Not insane	5	1	6							1		1
Totals	207	165	372	63	41	104	45	37	82	715	670	1,385

TABLE X.

SHOWING OCCUPATION OF MALE PATIENTS ADMITTED DURING YEAR ENDING NOVEMBER 15, 1898.

Occupation.	No.
Baker	1
Barber	1
Bookkeepers	3
Butchers	2
Blacksmiths	3
Brakeman	1
Brick masons	2
Carpenters	8
Cook	1
Cigar maker	1
Clerks	5
Contractor	1
Coopers	2
Druggist	1
Farmers	61
Gardeners	2
Insurance agent	1
Laborers	59
Lawyer	1
Lighthouse-keeper	1
Machinists	6
Merchants	6
Miners	2
Minister	1
Mechanics	5
Moulder	1
Musician	1
Painter	1
Physicians	2
Plasterer	1
Printer	1
Railroad engineers	3
Sailors	2
Saloon keeper	1
Shoemaker	1
Students	8
Telegraph operator	1
Teachers	3
Tinners	4
Traveling salesman	1
Veterinarian	1
Unknown	3
Total	207

TABLE XI.

SHOWING NATIVITY OF PATIENTS ADMITTED DURING THE YEAR ENDING NOVEMBER 15, 1898, AND OF THOSE ADMITTED SINCE OPENING OF THE INSTITUTION.

United States.	During year.			Since opening of institution.		
	M.	W.	T.	M.	W.	T.
Arkansas				1		1
Connecticut				13	1	14
Delaware					1	1
Georgia				1		1
Illinois		1	1	4	9	13
Indiana	1	2	3	21	24	45
Iowa				3	8	11
Kentucky		2	2	4	10	14
Kansas					2	2
Louisiana				3	2	5
Maine					1	1
Maryland	1	1	2	20	8	28
Massachusetts				10	5	15
Michigan	4	3	7	33	21	54
Minnesota					1	1
Mississippi				2		2
Missouri	1		1	2	1	3
Nebraska					1	1
New Hampshire				2	1	3
New Jersey	1	1	2	8	8	16
New York	8	4	12	104	83	187
North Carolina	1		1	6		6
Ohio	149	114	263	1,558	1,458	3,016
Pennsylvania	8	8	16	141	78	219
Rhode Island				1	1	2
Tennessee	1		1	2	3	5
Vermont				3	3	6
Virginia	1	2	3	16	10	26
West Virginia		1	1	9	4	13
Wisconsin				1	2	3
Totals	176	139	315	1,968	1,746	3,714
Foreign Countries.						
Austria				2	1	3
Belgium					1	1
Bavaria	1		1	4	1	5
Bohemia				1		1
Canada	1		1	29	25	54
Denmark				2		2
England	2	4	6	45	30	75
Finland				1		1
France	1	2	3	8	11	19
Germany	14	10	24	282	244	526
Hungary				1	3	4
Holland				2		2
Ireland	2	2	4	73	77	150
Italy				2		2
Jersey Isle				1		1
New Brunswick	1		1	2		2
Norway	1		1	2		2

TABLE XI—Concluded.

Foreign Countries.	During year.			Since opening of institution.		
	M.	W.	T.	M.	W.	T.
Ocean born	1		1	2		2
Poland				6	5	11
Prince Edward Island		1	1	2	1	3
Prussia				5	2	7
Russia		1	1	6	2	8
Rock of Gibraltar				1		1
Scotland				3	9	12
Sweden		1	1	4	3	7
Switzerland	3	1	4	36	22	58
Wales				5	4	9
Unknown	4	4	8	70	75	145
Totals	31	26	57	597	516	1,113
Total United States	176	139	315	1,968	1,746	3,714
Total Foreign Countries	31	26	57	597	516	1,113
Grand totals	207	165	372	2,565	2,262	4,827

TABLE XII.

SHOWING QUOTA AND THE NUMBER OF PATIENTS EACH COUNTY HAS IN HOSPITAL ON THE 15TH DAY OF NOVEMBER, 1898.

Toledo State Hospital district.	M.	W.	T.	Quota.
Allen	39	22	61	49
Ashland	18	16	34	27
Auglaize	18	23	41	35
Crawford	25	17	42	39
Defiance	16	17	33	32
Erie	29	33	62	44
Fulton	18	18	36	27
Hancock	30	35	65	52
Hardin	23	21	44	36
Henry	21	20	41	31
Huron	18	30	48	39
Lorain	31	32	63	49
Lucas	108	99	207	126
Mercer	23	16	39	33
Ottawa	20	14	34	27
Paulding	25	12	37	32
Putnam	26	14	40	37
Richland	26	33	59	47
Sandusky	25	26	51	38
Seneca	31	37	68	50
Stark	1	2	3	....
Van Wert	21	21	42	36
Wayne	25	30	55	48
Williams	16	14	30	31
Wood	34	29	63	55
Wyandot	25	13	38	27
Total Toledo district	692	644	1,386	1,047
Other Districts.				
Ashtabula	1	1	2	....
Cuyahoga	16	16	32	....
Columbiana	3	7	10	....
Darke	1	....	1	....
Hamilton	1	1	2	....
Mahoning	....	1	1	....
Montgomery	1	....	1	....
Total other districts	28	26	49	....
Total Toledo district	692	644	1,336	1,047
Total other districts	23	26	49	....
Grand totals	715	670	1,385	1,047

TABLE XIII.

SHOWING DAILY AVERAGE NUMBER OF PATIENTS WALKING OUTSIDE, EMPLOYED, ETC., FOR EACH MONTH,

Months.	Walking outside.						Employed at—												Attended.					
	Unattended.			Attended.			Laundry, kitchen and dining room.			Ward work.			Sewing room and fancy work.			Barn, farm and grounds.			Amusements and chapel.			General dining room.		
	M.	W.	T.	M.	W.	T.	M.	W.	T.	M.	W.	T.	M.	W.	T.	M.	W.	T.	M.	W.	T.	M.	W.	T.
December	143	84	227	405	387	792	70	82	102	181	186	367		20	20	18		18	257	214	471	420	354	774
January	142	80	222	366	361	727	70	28	98	181	186	367		17	17	18		18	235	162	397	424	351	775
February	141	77	218	373	360	733	68	29	97	181	186	367		21	21	19		19	164	119	283	428	342	770
Mch	152	77	229	371	368	739	68	29	97	181	186	367		20	20	23		23	218	125	338	482	340	772
April	151	88	237	400	405	805	67	30	97	182	186	368		22	22	28		28	241	163	404	488	315	778
May	149	93	242	395	399	794	68	29	97	182	185	368		20	20	39		39	136	81	217	429	347	776
June	147	101	248	400	419	819	68	41	109	181	176	357		16	16	55		55	370	150	446	430	346	776
July	151	108	259	390	440	830	69	56	128	181	171	352		12	12	46		46	313	122	492	434	342	786
August	150	109	259	385	441	826	67	42	111	181	176	357		16	16	45		45	313	126	489	429	364	793
September	143	94	237	375	426	801	69	44	106	181	181	362		13	13	45		45	254	92	346	412	353	798
tober	129	84	213	336	387	728	60	51	111	181	181	362		16	16	43		43	184	73	207	381	349	730
eber	132	91	228	326	396	721	64	38	92	181	181	362		40	40	87		87	143	85	228	384	261	745

STEWARD'S ANNUAL REPORT.

TOLEDO STATE HOSPITAL, TOLEDO, OHIO, November 15, 1898.

H. A. TOBEY, M. D., Superintendent:

DEAR SIR: I herewith submit the fifteenth annual report of the financial department of this institution, for the fiscal year ending November 15, 1898.

Respectfully,

C. S. MILLER,
Financial Officer.

STATEMENT

Showing conditions of the various appropriations with the State Treasury for the fiscal year ending November 15, 1898.

Name of appropriation.	Balance in State Treasury November 15, 1897.	Appropriations made during the year ending November 15, 1898.	Total amount subject to draft during the fiscal year.	Amount drawn from the State Treasury for the year ending November 15, 1898.	Balance in the State Treasury November 15, 1898.
Current expenses	$55,445 41	$171,750 00	$227,195 41	$161,504 64	$65,690 77
Salaries of officers and trustees' expenses	815 73	6,682 00	7,497 73	6,009 98	1,487 75
Ordinary repairs etc.	4,806 65	21,250 00	25,556 65	17,124 21	8,432 44
Disposal of sewage	215 28		215 28	215 28	
Kitchen, etc.		5,000 00	5,000 00	4,364 56	635 45
Enlarging and remodeling cottages		11,000 00	11,000 00	10,998 95	6 05
Sewage storage tank and completing beds		4,000 00	4,000 00	2,259 89	1,740 11
Elevator for boiler house		500 00	500 00	500 00	
Addition to laundry building and machinery		5,560 00	5,560 00	5,500 00	
Furnishing and equipping "L" building		5,000 00	5,000 00	5,000 00	
Totals	$60,788 07	$230,682 00	$291,465 07	$218,472 50	$77,992 57

STATEMENT

Showing balances on hand November 15, 1897, amounts received from State Treasury and all other sources, and amounts disbursed during the fiscal year and balance in hands of financial officer November 15, 1898.

Name of appropriation.	Balance on hand November 15, 1897.	Received from State Treasury.	Received from counties.	Received from miscellaneous sales, discounts, etc.	Totals to be accounted for.	Amounts disbursed during the year.	Balance in hands of financial officer November 15, 1898.
Current expenses	$766 27	$161,504 64	$17,581 61	$1,087 56	$180,839 08	$180,733 00	$106 08
Salaries of officers and trustees' expenses		6,009 98			6,009 98	6,009 98	
Ordinary repairs, etc		17,124 21			17,124 21	17,124 21	
Disposal of sewage		215 28			215 28	215 28	
Kitchen, etc		4,364 55			4,364 55	4,364 55	
Enlarging and remodeling cottages		10,993 95			10,993 95	10,993 95	
Sewage storage tank and completing beds		2,259 89			2,259 89	2,259 89	
Elevator for boiler house		500 00			500 00	500 00	
Addition to laundry building and machinery		5,500 00			5,500 00	5,500 00	
Finishing and equipping "L" building		5,000 00			5,000 00	5,000 00	
Totals	$765 27	$218,472 50	$17,581 61	$1,087 56	$232,906 94	$232,700 86	$106 08

RECEIPTS AND DISBURSEMENTS OF CURRENT EXPENSES OF THE
TOLEDO STATE HOSPITAL FOR THE FISCAL YEAR ENDING
NOVEMBER 15, 1898.

On what account.	Amount.	Total.
Receipts.		
Balance on hand November 15, 1897	$765 27	
Received from State Treasury	161,505 64	
" auditors of counties.....................................	17,531 61	
" miscellaneous sales	683 78	
" shoemaker	102 69	
" operator	37 41	
" discounts	148 46	
" sale of products......	65 22	
		$180,839 08
Disbursements.		
Amusements	$986 01	
Boots and shoes.......	1,677 16	
Butter and eggs	13,414 38	
Breadstuffs	8,124 69	
Blacksmithing	147 30	
Blank books and stationery	476 17	
Brooms and brushes	445 15	
Chapel services	206 38	
Cutlery..	148 77	
Cider and vinegar.......	172 33	
Candies and nuts..............	118 63	
Canned goods..............	766 58	
Clothing and furnishing	10,749 78	
Drugs and medicines	2,078 17	
Dry goods and notions......	7,333 68	
Dried and evaporated fruits	2,300 27	
Electrical supplies	243 83	
Freight and express	733 20	
Forage	315 78	
Fuel and light	13,408 64	
Fish and oysters	1,353 28	
Fresh fruits and berries...........................	969 12	
Groceries...............	14,811 81	
Hardware	417 40	
Laundry supplies....., ...	1,189 57	
Milk..........	8,424 67	
Meats and lard..	25,683 21	
Oils......	332 75	
Postage	487 38	
Poultry and game.......................................	1,420 78	
Patients' expenses.......	1,218 49	
Plants and seeds	262 11	
Queensware and glassware	581 25	
Repairs	22 78	
Surgical supplies.......................................	37 90	
Shoemaker supplies	296 90	

RECEIPTS AND DISBURSEMENTS—Concluded.

On what account.	Amount.	Total.
Disbursements—Concluded.		
Tobaccos	$1,128 72	
Telegraph and telephone	392 46	
Traveling expenses	610 41	
Vegetables	2,724 11	
Wooden and willowware	130 03	
Wines and liquors	368 36	
Wages, male	34,097 94	
" female	17,937 88	
Miscellaneous	1,992 29	
		$180,733 00
Balance in hands of financial officer		106 06
		$180,839 06

CURRENT EXPENSES.

'On what account.	Amount.	Total.
Amusements.		
Athletic games	$13 50	
Base balls, 36	32 18	
Boats, 3	72 50	
Ball bats, 24	10 50	
Baritone horn, 1	20 00	
Burnt cork, 6 boxes	1 50	
Band music, 31 selections	37 97	
Bass viol, 1	25 00	
Cello strings 6	2 47	
Checker boards, 6	2 00	
Circus	45 25	
Checkers, 1 dozen	65	
Clarinet reeds, 1½ dozen	3 60	
Croquet sets, 2	1 50	
Chess boards, 1 dozen	75	
Cards, playing, 3⅓ gross	37 00	
Cue tips, 7 boxes	3 55	
Christmas expenses	95	
Drum head, 1	3 25	
Dominos, 1⁷⁄₁₂ dozen	1 15	
Entertainments, 7	151 55	
Flags, 18 dozen	7 10	
Fireworks	50 55	
Fish hooks	26	
Fish lines, 1 gross	1 50	
Masks, 5 dozen	4 75	
Mouth piece, 1	1 50	
Orchestra music	38 50	
Rosin, 1 box	20	
Special street cars	6 00	
Score books, 3	91	
State Hospital orchestra	354 42	
Transportation to Fair	6 25	
Vocal music	37 89	
Violin strings, 4 bundles	8 86	
Indicator, 1	50	$986 01
Boots and Shoes.		
Boots, leather, 12 pairs	$23 00	
" rubber, 19 "	37 86	
Rubbers, women's, 64 pairs	22 09	
Shoes, men's, 433 pairs	495 70	
" women's, 679 pairs	747 30	
Slippers, women's, 181 pairs	100 01	
" men's, 314 pairs	251 20	1,677 16
Butter and Eggs.		
Butter, creamery, 38,917 pounds	$7,119 30	
" dairy, 17,019 pounds	2,644 67	
Eggs, 31,164 dozen	3,650 41	13,414 38
Breadstuffs.		
Buckwheat flour, 2 barrels	$9 00	
Crackers, 11,329 pounds	625 45	

CURRENT EXPENSES—Continued.

On what account.	Amount.	Total.
Breadstuffs—Concluded.		
Cornmeal, 17,540 pounds..	$142 40	
Flour, 1,884 barrels.........	7,273 47	
Graham flour, 7 barrels	29 05	
Wafers, 21 pounds.......	2 49	
Yeast, 52 pounds	13 00	
Zephyrettes, 286¾ pounds	29 83	
		$8,124 69
Blacksmithing.		
Shoeing horses and repairs..	....	147 30
Blank Books and Stationery.		
Arnold's writing fluid, 12¼ quarts..	$5 38	
Articles required for 17,200..	27 75	
Admission cards, 5,000..	5 50	
Blotters, ½ dozen	20	
Blank books, 21..	27 85	
" reports, 1,200...	8 00	
Carbon paper, 2 boxes	3 50	
Cards, 1,000..	2 50	
Coin envelopes, 2,000...	1 50	
Clothing records, 2,000	8 50	
Diamond paste	50	
Daily store orders	3 50	
Dating stamp, 1...	25	
Examination blanks, 500...	4 00	
Erasers, 12...	80	
Envelopes, 1,000	1 60	
Fillers, ½ dozen	90	
Glass pens, ½ dozen	1 50	
Index pads, 2 sets	3 25	
Indelible ink, 4 pounds	37 50	
Ink, 21 dozen	5 30	
Journals, 3	1 80	
Ledgers, 2	80	
Letter brush, 1..	40	
Mucilage, 112 dozen...	6 20	
Memo's, 2..	1 20	
Mathews' memo. pads, 1 gross	8 10	
McGill's fasteners, 400..	60	
Morocco covers, 3	1 75	
Noteheads, 20,000	51 00	
Printing..	8 35	
Paste, 2 bottles ....:	50	
Pencils, 6⅓ gross..	7 45	
Point protectors, 2 dozen	50	
Paper, 1 M	75	
Pens, 22 gross...	11 55	
Penholders, 1 dozen	60	
Programs, 2,100..	23 50	
Postal cards, 1,550............	18 25	
Pad, 1...............	15	
Receipt book, 1	25	
Rubber stamp, 1	30	
Rulers, ⅓ dozen	55	

CURRENT EXPENSES—Continued.

On what account.	Amount.	Total.
		⌐
Blank Books and Stationery—Concluded.		
Rubber bands, 1 box..	$0 75	
Records, 12	10 14	
Sponge cups, 2	20	
Shorthand pads, 2 dozen	1 00	
Supervisor's books, 2....................................	14 00	
Storekeeper receipts, 3,000............................	3 75	
Tissue paper, 1,000 sheets	1 85	
Shelf " 4 reams...............................	7 00	
Twine, 10 packages.......................................	5 00	
Typewriter, 1..	70 00	
Toilet paper, 2 case	14 00	
Typewriter paper, 1 box	90	
" ribbons, 3...............................	2 50	
Vouchers, 3,000	9 75	
Ward reports, 1,000......................................	7 75	
Writing paper, 29½ reams	21 94	
Wrapping paper, 4 "	1 03	
Photo supplies	10 28	
		$476 17
Brooms and Brushes.		
Brooms, ceiling, 1 dozen...............................	$2 40	
" barn, 1 dozen	3 25	
" carpet, 155 dozen............................	203 50	
" whisk, 35 dozen	23 00	
Brushes, hair, 14¾ dozen...............................	71 00	
" clothes, 3 "	9 00	
" bath, 4 "	8 70	
" scrub. 3½ gross..............................	40 00	
" shoe, ⅓ "	6 50	
" shaving, 2 dozen	4 50	
" tooth, 2 gross................................	13 30	
		445 15
Chapel Services.		
Services		206 38
Cutlery.		
Butcher knives, 5	$1 67	
Clippers, 1 pair	2 40	
Carvers, 2 sets..	5 50	
Carving forks, ½ dozen	2 25	
Knives and forks, 18 dozen.............................	66 00	
Razors, 1 dozen	9 00	
Shears, 5 "	25 23	
Teaspoons, 11 dozen.....................................	23 76	
Tablespoons, 3 "	12 96	
		148 77
Cider and Vinegar.		
Cider, 93 gallons	$11 62	
Vinegar, 2,069 gallons	160 71	
		172 33

CURRENT EXPENSES—Continued.

On what account.	Amount.	Total.
Candies and Nuts.		
Assorted candies, 868 pounds	$55 78	
Almonds, 10 pounds	2 30	
Assorted nuts, 120 pounds	11 60	
Dates, 14 pounds	1 81	
Figs, 17 "	2 04	
Peanuts, 812 pounds	44 67	
Walnuts, 5 pounds	48	
		$118 3
Canned Goods.		
Beans, 16 dozen	$14 60	
" 50 " gallons	200 00	
Corn, 336 "	289 60	
" 50 " gallons	175 00	
Mushrooms, 221 cans	43 79	
Ox tongue, ⅓ dozen	1 34	
Pumpkin, 4 dozen	2 50	
Peas, 14 dozen	19 00	
Sardines, 125 cans	24 00	
Salmon, 4 dozen	5 20	
Shrimp, 2 "	4 20	
Tomatoes, 27½ dozen	27 85	
Apples, 1 dozen	2 50	
Asparagus, 2 dozen	7 00	
		766 58
Clothing and Furnishing.		
Collars, paper, 9,700	$96 21	
Coats and vests, 76	69 05	
Caps, 242	86 13	
Drawers, women's, 2 dozen	4 50	
" men's, 23 dozen	92 76	
Fascinators, 284	118 83	
Gloves, 11½ dozen	41 10	
Gossamers, 104	179 20	
Hats, men's, 478	344 13	
Hats and trimmings, 740	249 48	
Hose, men's, 352½ dozen	270 44	
Hose, women's, 277¼ dozen	335 89	
Jumpers, 36	13 50	
Mittens, 4 dozen	18 50	
Neckties, 23¾ dozen	86 40	
Overcoats, 16	75 00	
Overalls, 150 pairs	57 00	
Pants, 402 pairs	615 45	
Pants and vests, 55 7/12 dozen	213 98	
Rubber coats, 344	1,107 60	
" tissue, 1 pound	1 25	
Suits, 799	4,990 85	
Shawls, 122	879 25	
Shirts and drawers, 104½ dozen	869 68	
Shirts, 136⅔ dozen	553 21	
Suspenders, 68 7/12 dozen	130 78	
Ties, 86¼ dozen	90 28	
Under shirts, 15½ dozen	57 13	
Vests, 54 dozen	157 75	
		10,749 78

CURRENT EXPENSES—Continued.

On what account.	Amount.	Total.
Drugs and Medicines.		
Alcohol, 49¼ gallons..	$122 10	
Absorbent cotton, 475 pounds............................	22 40	
Chloride lime, 462 pounds.................................	12 70	
Drugs and medicines.......................................	1,858 47	
Drug envelopes, 3,000.....................................	19 75	
Gauze, 500 yards..	11 25	
Malted milk, 75 pounds....................................	30 00	
Poison labels, 5,000..	1 50	
		$2,078 17
Dry Goods and Notions.		
Agate buttons, 10¾ gross..................................	$12 87	
Buttons, pants, 1 gt.gross.................................	65	
" coat, 4 gross	2 70	
" collar, 51 dozen..................................	20 56	
" dress, 267⅓ gross...............................	147 77	
" vest, 4 gross......................................	1 62	
Blankets, rubber, 150.......................................	150 00	
" wool, 228..	412 40	
Cambric, 538¾ yards.......................................	16 40	
Canton flannel, 1,217½ yards............................	92 83	
Cheese cloth, 877½ yards..................................	14 15	
Combs, 118 1/12 dozen.....................................	76 60	
Corsets, 12 1/12 dozen....................................	65 00	
Corset laces, 16 gross......................................	10 20	
Crepe, 9 rolls..	1 28	
Corset steels, 8 gross......................................	5 60	
Crash, 4,989 yards...	388 05	
Crochet hooks, 1 gross.....................................	1 75	
Curtains, lace, 5..	6 25	
Chambray, 27 yards..	2 70	
Cord, rubber, 22 dozen.....................................	9 65	
Cotton batting, 3,305 pounds.............................	283 70	
Diaper cloth, 258 yards....................................	22 06	
Ducking, 868 yards...	28 93	
Darning cotton, 7 boxes....................................	1 30	
Denims, 700 yards..	71 80	
Drain cloth, 50 yards.......................................	8 75	
Dress goods, 2,140¼ yards................................	281 32	
Elastic web, 8 dozen.......................................	33 55	
Fans, 500...	4 50	
Feather dusters, 4½ dozen................................	11 12	
Flannel, 1,541¾ yards.....................................	251 43	
Gingham, 4,723¾ yards....................................	250 68	
Handkerchiefs, 229 dozen.................................	104 40	
Hooks and eyes, 1 gross...................................	2 00	
Hair pins, 96 packages.....................................	13 90	
Knitting cotton, 108 pounds..............................	38 06	
Linen, 654½ yards..	272 59	
Machine needles, 525.......................................	7 04	
Mosquito netting, 57 pieces...............................	18 10	
Muslin, 12,762¾ yards.....................................	750 78	
Napkins, 68 dozen..	105 00	
Needles, sewing, 20⅝ M...................................	28 17	
" darning, 2¼ M..................................	1 85	
Oil cloth, 4 rolls..	5 00	

CURRENT EXPENSES—Continued.

On what account.	Amount.	Total.
Dry Goods and Notions—Concluded.		
Prints, 13,673½ yards	$595 61	
Pearl buttons, 2 gross	. 2 30	
Pins, 63 dozen	18 76	
" safety, 27 gross	11 15	
Sheeting, 5,888 yards	525 69	
Silesia, 441¼ yards	37 11	
Scrim, 128½ "	9 64	
Shoe laces, 52 gross	21 63	
Shirting, 10,334½ yards	591 18	
Spectacles, 2 pair	7 00	
Spreads, bed, 172	135 40	
Stays, 6 boxes	5 10	
Stay binding, 15 gross	6 75	
Table linen, 867½ yards	406 76	
" felt, 1½ yards	60	
Tape, 68 dozen	9 52	
Thimbles, 5 gross	6 25	
Table cloths, 2	13 00	
Twist, 18 boxes	6 75	
Tape linen, 1 dozen	37	
Tri-State gingham, 1,661¾ yards	112 95	
Thread, cotton, 630 dozen	·268 11	
" silk, 4 dozen	1 50	
" carpet, 9 dozen	8 10	
Ticking, 3,769 yards	349 96	
Towels, 76⅔ dozen	104 53	
Umbrellas, 1 dozen	4 80	
White goods, 210 yards	17 52	
Ribbon, 22 bolts	26 08	
		$7,333 68
Dried and Evaporated Fruits.		
Apples, evaporated, 3,150 pounds	$227 88	
Apricots, " 5,008 "	364 78	
Currants, 511 pounds	85 77	
Citron, 20 pounds	2 50	
Figs, 23 "	2 02	
Peaches, evaporated, 11,327 pounds	839 91	
Prunes, 11,835 pounds	664 82	
Raisins, 4,483 "	161 09	
" sugar, 14 pounds	1 50	
		2,300 27
Electrical Supplies.		
Lamps, 1,325	$231 50	
Manhattan globes, 12	3 00	
Mica chimney, 1	1 15	
Mantles, 6	2 10	
Supplies	6 08	
		243 83
Freight and Express.		
Freight and express		733 20

On what account.	Amount.	Total.
Forage.		
Bran, 2,000 pounds	$13 00	
Oats, 508 bushels	163 72	
Straw, 49,475 pounds	139 06	$315 78
Fuel and Light.		
Blossburg coal, 5,730 pounds	$12 67	
Coal, lump, 7,865½ tons	10,677 87	
Charcoal, 104½ bushels	17 36	
Gasoline, 361 gallons	26 59	
Gas, fuel	2,668 65	
Gas tank, 1	5 50	
		13,408 64
Fish and Oysters.		
Fish, fresh, 29,127½ pounds	$870 94	
" Cod 2 barrels	15 00	
Mackerel, 11 barrels	188 50	
Oysters, bulk, 240 gallons	197 40	
" canned, 228½ cans	81 44	
		1,353 28
Fresh Fruits and Berries.		
Apples, 109½ barrels	$118 18	
Apricots, ½ bushel	1 75	
Blue.berries, ½ bushel	1 25	
Bananas, 20 bunches	26 25	
Crab apples, 3 bushels	3 00	
Cranberries, 16½ bushels	53 00	
Cherries, 21½ bushels	36 83	
Grapes, 79 baskets	11 16	
" 2 kegs	14 00	
" 2 barrels	8 00	
" 2 cases	3 00	
" 5,677 pounds	52 49	
Lettuce, 5 pounds	40	
Lemons, 36 boxes	170 25	
Oranges, 45 "	159 33	
Pineapples, 8 dozen	13 00	
Pears, 125½ bushels	64 18	
Plums, 1 crate	1 40	
" 11 baskets	6 35	
" 15½ bushels	23 50	
Peaches, 8½ crates	14 60	
" 5 baskets	2 15	
" 171¼ bushels	135 85	
Quinces, 9 bushels	7 70	
Strawberries, 18 cases	41 50	
		969 12
Groceries.		
Allspice, 40 pounds	$4 60	
Apple butter, 2,786 pounds	105 82	
Barley, 925 pounds	22 88	
Beans, 21,705 pounds	436 86	
" Lima, 1,929 pounds	58 05	

CURRENT EXPENSES—Continued.

On what account.	Amount.	Total.
Groceries—Continued.		
Baking powder, 84 pounds................................	$81 86	
Cinnamon, 55 pounds...................................	12 90	
Catsup, 10 dozen.....................................	22 40	
Crayon, 1 dozen........................	96	
Cocoanut, 20 pounds..................................	2 40	
Chocolate, 74 pounds.................................	23 82	
Cocoa, 12 pounds	5 52	
Cheese, 10,765 pounds	1,017 63	
Coffee, 32,351 pounds................................	3,971 38	
Cloves, 45 pounds....................................	4 80	
Cream tartar, 824½ pounds............................	215 65	
Celery seed, 2 pounds	30	
Corn starch, 1,200 pounds	48 00	
Dressing, 2 boxes	8 80	
Extracts, 8 gallons	44 00	
Edam cheese, 9	8 31	
Fly paper, 5 boxes...................................	11 40	
Figs, 1 box	85	
Gelatine, 9 dozen	14 00	
Glucose, 153 pounds..................................	4 51	
Ginger, 40 pounds...................................	4 80	
Hominy, 14 barrels...................................	32 55	
Hops, 18 pounds....................................	5 40	
Horseradish, 74½ gallons.............................	37 25	
Kleanit, ½ gross	4 00	
Kerosene, 831 gallons................................	45 53	
Worcestershire sauce, 1 dozen........................	4 75	
Macaroni, 25 pounds..................................	2 50	
Malt, 75 pounds.....................................	3 75	
Mustard, 5 kegs	8 75	
" 2 dozen......	5 50	
" seed, 4 pounds................................	36	
Maple syrup, 10 cases................................	47 50	
Matches, 2 cases....................................	32 00	
Molasses, 1,157 gallons..............................	171 39	
N. O. molasses, 158 gallons...........................	25 74	
Nutmegs, 5 pounds...................................	2 25	
Olives, 7 gallons....................................	6 50	
Oats, rolled, 11 barrels...............................	40 25	
Oatmeal, 26 barrels..................................	102 33	
Paraffine, 215 pounds	13 98	
Pipes, 5 boxes......................................	7 15	
Paper, 571 pounds...................................	8 87	
" sacks, 2½ M.................................	4 18	
Pickles, 64 gallons...................................	33 50	
Pepper, 300 pounds..................................	29 00	
" sauce, 6	68	
Rice, 4 885 pounds...................................	242 92	
Sapolio, 18½ gross	163 13	
Shoe polish, 9 dozen.................................	5 70	
Stove " 2½ gross	17 80	
Salad dressing, 3 dozen	9 40	
Soda, bi carbonate, 672 pounds........................	18 20	
Shelled almonds, 48 pounds	11 60	
Soap, shaving, 110 pounds............................	27 50	
" toilet, 14 dozen	8 98	

CURRENT EXPENSES—Continued.

On what account.	Amount.	Total.
Groceries—Concluded.		
Salt, 68 barrels..	$54 32	
Soap, toilet, 34 boxes	145 25	
" laundry, 117 boxes.......................	238 75	
Sugar, cut loaf, 507 pounds............................	30 26	
" A, 347 pounds	17 62	
" granulated, 110,084 pounds..........	5,907 60	
" powdered, 796 pounds	49 87	
Sage, 10 pounds..	1 00	
Tea, 4,020 pounds	1,043 61	
Twine, 124 pounds...	12 25	
Toothpicks, 3 cases	5 56	
Tapioca, 453 pounds	13 93	
Wheat flake, 1 box	3 00	
Wicking, 5 pounds	80	
Soap powder, 302 pounds................................	30 20	$14,811 81
Hardware.		
Ax, 1...	$0 54	
Bolts, 620...	36	
Broad hatchet, 1	65	
Brass screws, 5 gross	65	
" 16½ pounds	1 04	
Butter molds, 1 dozen......................................	35	
Coffee boilers, ¾ dozen....................................	1 70	
Carpet sweepers, 2..	4 00	
Copper bottom chambers, 6 dozen......................	32 40	
Castors, 7 sets...	5 78	
Chains, key, 2 dozen	2 00	
Dust pans, 12 dozen	14 40	
Egg beaters, 3...	68	
File, 1	20	
Glass, 1 light..	1 07	
Glue, 20 pounds...	2 20	
Hoes, 1 dozen..	3 00	
Handles, 4½ dozen...	4 48	
Hose, 200 feet...	20 00	
Hollow mandrill, 1...	3 71	
Iron, 548 pounds...	6 96	
Key blanks, ¾ dozen	57	
Key rings, 6 dozen...	1 20	
Kettles, 6...	9 65	
Lanterns, 1 dozen	4 00	
Mantles, 4	1 60	
Nuts, 10 pounds..	33	
Picture nails, ¼ gross	50	
" cord, 1 dozen...........................	75	
Nails, 9 kegs	14 10	
Pig lead, 82 pounds	8 49	
Pictures, 1 gross..	3 65	
Pruning saw, 1..	50	
Pulleys, ¼ dozen...	07	
Rakes, ½ dozen...	2 00	
Razor strops, 30	14 80	
Roasting pans, 2	7 00	
Rule, 1...	17	

CURRENT EXPENSES—Continued.

On what account.	Amount.	Total.
Hardware—Concluded.		
Steak pans, 17	$2 55	
Saw blade, 1	50	
Shovels, 6	60	
Solder, 200 pounds	22 64	
Sledge handles, 2 dozen	2 50	
Soup ladles, 3 dozen	1 59	
Shovels, 3½ dozen	26 13	
Scythes, ₁⁵₂ "	2 25	
Snaths, 2¼ "	1 76	
Scythe stones, 1 dozen	75	
Screws, 1 gross	1 56	
Staples, 10 pounds	45	
Tureens, 2 dozen	32 40	
Tubing, 8 feet	40	
Tea strainers, ½ dozen	33	
Tin, 25 boxes	126 00	
Tin pails, 4 dozen	7 00	
Wire cloth, 750 square feet	7 50	
Waffle irons, 2	3 14	
Wheelbarrows, ⅓ dozen	4 50	
Washers, 10 pounds	30	
Wire scoops	2 00	
		$417 40
Laundry Supplies.		
Bluing, 2½ gross	$14 75	
Caustic soda, 7,465 pounds	204 81	
Chipped soap, 12,919 pounds	485 13	
Starch, 6,053 pounds	163 13	
Soap, laundry, 150 boxes	321 75	
		1,189 57
Milk.		
Milk, 77,465 gallons		8,424 67
Meats and Lard.		
Bacon, 12,460 pounds	$902 28	
Beef, 185,614 pounds	13,892 23	
Corned beef, 33,419 pounds	1,313 89	
Dried beef, 5,638 pounds	745 94	
Frankfurts, 5,050 "	321 82	
Ham, 55,055 pounds	3,944 61	
Lard, 11,520 "	648 17	
Lamb, 964 "	86 89	
Liver, 9,576 "	191 40	
Mutton, 8,580 "	567 96	
Ox tongues, smoked, 100 pounds	14 50	
Pork, fresh, 4,982 pounds	249 10	
" salt, 25 barrels	235 25	
Suet, 100 pounds	4 00	
Sausage, 18,080 pounds	1,015 62	
Sweet breads, 1₁⁵₆ pounds	30	
Tongues, 89 pounds	30 88	
Veal, 17,495 "	1,518 37	
		25,683 21

CURRENT EXPENSES—Continued.

On what account.	Amount.	Total.
Oils.		
Cylinder, 369½ gallons	$167 06	
Dynamo, 257½ "	67 11	
Lard, 10 gallons	5 25	
Paraffine, 203 pounds	13 19	
Olive, 1 case	6 00	
Sewing machine, 36	2 05	
Turpentine, 105 gallons	30 46	
T., S., P., 502 pounds	32 63	
		$332 75
Postage.		
Envelopes, stamped, 19,000	$415 28	
Stamps, revenue	5 00	
"	67 10	
		487 38
Poultry and Game.		
Chickens, alive, 206 pounds	$21 01	
" " 9 dozen	29 65	
" dressed, 9,108	768 93	
Ducks, 71 pounds	6 95	
Quail, 5⅛ dozen	12 80	
Squabs, 4 "	6 60	
Turkeys, 4,948½ pounds	557 51	
Frogs, 53 dozen	8 45	
Mallards, 16½ dozen	8 88	
		1,420 78
Patients' Expenses.		
Labor	$648 61	
Transferring patients to Massillon	290 71	
Returning escapes	221 89	
Teeth, 1 set	15 00	
Traveling, sent home	42 78	
		1,218 49
Plants and Seeds.		
Plants and seeds		262 11
Queensware and Glassware.		
Bakers, 50 dozen	$99 87	
Basins, 1 "	4 28	
Bowls, 4 "	4 86	
" sugar, 3¾ dozen	8 25	
Chambers, 4 dozen	12 80	
Creamers, ⅓ "	94	
Can caps, 1½ gross	3 13	
Chimneys, 2 cases	3 00	
Cups, 75½ dozen	59 49	
Cuspidors, ⅔ dozen	4 83	
Cups and saucers, 45 dozen	39 99	
Dishes, 4 dozen	8 66	
Ewers, 27	18 00	
Globes, 1 dozen	1 80	
Invalid plates, 6	5 10	

CURRENT EXPENSES—Continued.

On what account.	Amount.	Total.
Queensware and Glassware—Concluded.		
Invalid cups, 12	$1 50	
Jelly cans, 30 dozen	5 40	
Lantern globes, 1 dozen	45	
Molasses jugs, 3 dozen	4 50	
Mason jars, 21 dozen	12 11	
Mugs, shaving, 2 dozen	1 50	
Nappies, $\frac{7}{12}$ dozen	1 08	
Oyster bowls, 24 dozen	24 48	
Plates, 89½ dozen	79 82	
Pitchers, 252	41 21	
Pickle dishes, ½ dozen	1 13	
Platters, 2 dozen	10 80	
Salt and peppers, 6 dozen	2 16	
Sauce dishes, ¼ dozen	2 63	
Saucers, 36 dozen	18 90	
Scallops, 14½½ dozen	31 67	
Slop jars, 1½ dozen	9 67	
Tumblers, 75$\frac{8}{12}$ dozen	33 27	
Vinegar cruets, 2⅓ dozen	4 67	
Vegetable dishes, 4 "	8 40	
Water pitchers, 3 "	4 30	
Whisky glasses, 1 "	45	
Spoons, 1 dozen	65	
Water coolers, 2	5 50	
		$581 25
Repairs.		
Glasses, 2 pair	$0 25	
Horn	14 25	
Machines	8 28	
		22 78
Surgical Supplies.		
Surgical supplies		37 90
Shoemakers' Supplies.		
Awls, 1	$0 15	
Blocks, 3 dozen	13 40	
Buttons, 1 great gross	35	
Bristles, 1 ounce	1 10	
Button fasteners, 5 M	2 60	
Buffer, 1	10	
Calf skin, 2⅛⅛ pounds	2 55	
Cement, 9 pints	3 40	
Cordovan shank, 1 piece	58	
Dressing, ½ dozen	50	
Dye, 5 bottles	2 25	
Emery paper, ⅓ dozen	05	
Heel lifts, 18 dozen	8 32	
" balls, 4 "	18	
Ink, 2 bottles	40	
Insoles, cork, 1 dozen	60	
" leather, 1 piece	22	
Lining	50	
Lasts, 4 pair	1 00	

CURRENT EXPENSES—Continued.

On what account.	Amount.	Total.
Shoemakers' Supplies—Concluded.		
Lifts, 17 dozen	$9 64	
Nippers, 36 pounds..............................	2 62	
Nails, 113 pounds	6 90	
Oak block, 6 dozen	25 15	
Patches, kid, 7 pounds........................	2 15	
Plates, 30 boxes	8 64	
Rubber patches, 4⅛ pounds..................	1 70	
Rubber, 4 squares	1 54	
" cement, 2 pints	60	
Shoe knives, 3....................................	1 03	
Sand paper, ½ dozen	05	
Skirting, 10½ pounds..........................	1 53	
Seam fastener....................................	2 50	
Sole leather, 148¾ pounds	33 86	
Silk, 1 spool	50	
Stretchers, 2......................................	3 20	
Soap stone	05	
Shanks, 15	28	
Taps, 116 dozen	152 29	
Thread, 7..	8 40	
Till	35	
Wax	10	
Welts	62	
		$296 90
Tobaccos.		
Stogies, 1,000....................................	$12 50	
Tobacco, chewing, 5,589 pounds............	1,009 12	
" smoking, 850 "	104 60	
Tobacco stems, 250 pounds	2 50	
		1,128 72
Telegraph and Telephone.		
City phone, 12 months	$138 00	
Tolls and messenger service	100 63	
Telegraph messages............................	153 83	
		392 46
Traveling Expenses.		
H. A. Tobey	$846 55	
R. E. Hamblin....................................	13 36	
C. S. Miller..	40 80	
F. A. Todd..	2 80	
W. G. Cooper	41 60	
Ves Enright	1 95	
F. J. Raab..	2 85	
F. A. Todd, treatment expenses............	160 50	
		610 41
Vegetables.		
Beans, 3 bushels..................................	$3 75	
Beets, 1 bushel	45	
Cabbage, 1 crate................................	1 25	
Cauliflower, 1 dozen	1 25	
Celery, 21 dozen................................	9 30	
Cucumbers, 21 dozen..........................	6 10	

CURRENT EXPENSES—Continued.

On what account.	Amount.	Total.
Vegetables—Concluded.		
Lettuce, 100 pounds..	$11 23	
Mushrooms..	75	
Muskmelons, 48..	2 75	
Peas, 1 bushel..	1 00	
Potatoes, sweet, 10 barrels...............	26 05	
" Irish, 3,847½ bushels	2,498 44	
Radishes, 8 dozen........	2 00	
Tomatoes, 8 bushels	11 09	
Watermelons, 1,755..........................	148 70	
		$2,724 11
Wooden and Willowware.		
Bowls, 2...	$1 00	
Butter molds, ½ dozen	38	
Clothes pins, 1 box	38	
" baskets, 12..	27 00	
Hampiers, 3	5 50	
Mop sticks, 3 gross	23 25	
Oak posts, 270	10 80	
Pails, 14 dozen...........................	18 90	
Spitoons, 9 dozen......................	32 10	
Slop jar mats, 1¾ dozen	3 94	
Tubs, 1 dozen............................	5 38	
Washboards, 1 dozen	1 40	
		130 03
Wines and Liquors.		
Beer, 2 dozen	$2 00	
Whisky, 125 gallons..	308 61	
Wine, 1½ case..................................	7 75	
Wine, 30 gallons	45 00	
		363 36
Wages—Male.		
Adams, F. J., attendant, 2 months, 28 days......	$76 25	
Andrews, George, dining room, 5 months, 27 days......	94 39	
Bennis, Chas., attendant, 8 days	7 20	
Bisling, Joseph, " 6 months ...	180 00	
Bentley, John, " 5 " 9 days.....	144 00	
Bell, W. J., " 12 "	324 00	
Brose, W. F., " 4 " 21 days.............	126 90	
Boden, W. W., " 12 "	343 00	
Breniff, D. J., " 6 " 16 days........	191 00	
Bryant, W. C., " 1 month, 4 "	38 00	
Burdsall, R. M., " 6 months, 21 "	178 90	
Brown, Albert, " 4 " 27 "	120 00	
Blasser, H. V., " 3 "	72 00	
Black, Emmett, " 2 " 28 days........	86 70	
Christiansen, Chris., attendant, 10 months, 12 days	325 50	
Crockett, S. H., " 5 " 1 day	151 00	
Cotter, Edw., barn, 12 months...	360 00	
Cook, W. A., dining room, 12 months........	360 00	
Cooper, W. G., " 12 "	100 00	
Carney, Merrell, " 11 " 8 days.........	180 26	
Condon, Wm., " 1 month, 26 "	47 70	
Conaway, C. J., " 9 months	150 60	

On what account.	Amount.	Total.
Wages—Male—Continued.		
Carney, N. G., engineer, 12 months	$1,000 00	
Casey, Arthur, fireman, 12 "	378 48	
Cooper, Jesse, kitchen, 12 "	241 00	
Collins, Edw., " 2 " 11 days	40 23	
Cropsey, C. E., attendant, 7 " 3 "	189 57	
Coon, R. R., tinner, 2 months	60 00	
Dunbar, C. E, attendant, 12 months	360 00	
Dowling, H. C., dining room 12 months	256 40	
Day, T. W., electrician, 8 " 9 days	370 00	
Davis, O., landscape gardener, 12 "	600 00	
DeTray, Henry, attendant, 2 " 28 days	76 26	
Douglas, Chas., kitchen, 5 "	85 00	
Dowling, M. J., attendant, 13 days	10 40	
Emsch. Benj., kitchen, 11 months, 24 days	265 10	
Elliott, Sherman, farm, 12 "	240 00	
Enright, Ves, carpenter, 12 "	565 00	
Eikert, E. F., plumber, 1 month, 23 days	63 00	
Ewing, Thomas, kitchen, 9 days	5 10	
Fish, George, attendant, 2 months, 26 days	69 66	
Frick, E. O., " 2 " 1 day	54 90	
Fitzgerald, Mike, laundry, 12 months	303 00	
Fletcher, Arthur, dining room, 3 days	1 60	
Fredericks, C. E., attendant, 4 months, 25 days	117 50	
Ferris, M. J., " 3 " 15 "	90 12	
Fluhart, Chas., kitchen, 5 " 16 "	100 11	
" Frank, " 2 " 1 day	34 57	
Gunn, A. G., attendant, 6 " 26 days	183 40	
Guile, C. G., " 11 " 25 "	302 83	
Geogline, Jacob, " 7 "	210 00	
Geer, R. P., " 9 " 29 days	270 10	
Garling Henry, " 2 "	60 00	
Gunning John, kitchen, 5 " 27 days	103 21	
Gunn, A. B., attendant, 4 " 26 "	128 52	
Gibson, Alex., kitchen, 26 days	14 71	
Horan, C. W., attendant, 8 months, 16 days	230 40	
Humphrey, J. N., " 5 " 21 "	153 90	
Hoge, L., " 10 " 29 "	329 00	
Horn, W. G., " 12 "	322 00	
Halsey, D. E., baker, 6 " 11 days	109 73	
Herold, Fred, cook, 12 "	600 00	
Harvey, Frank, dining room, 8 months	140 40	
Hight, Jesse, " 2 " 23 days	44 27	
Hannum, E. A., druggist, 12 "	600 00	
Hoge, Robt., fireman, 12 "	360 00	
Hamblin, R. E., Supt. G. and W. W., 5 months, 6 days	173 32	
" clerk, 5 months, 6 days	260 00	
Henmon, F. L., dining room, 1 month	16 00	
Hoge, Bert, " 6 months, 9 da s	100 80	
Harring, A. A., shoemaker, 12 " y	300 00	
Hisey, J. C., attendant, 9 " 11 days	281 00	
Hartman, Harry, " 5 " 14 "	127 81	
Kirkley, John, " 3 " 18 "	94 59	
Kelley, D. C, " 12 "	360 00	
Kirkpatrick, M. H., attendant, 11 months, 22 days	316 80	
King, W. C., night-watch, 11 months, 29 days	418 83	
Kelley, E. G., " 12 "	360 00	

CURRENT EXPENSES—Continued.

On what account.	Amount.	Total.
*Wages—Male—*Continued.		
Kingsbury, O. V., night-watch, 12 months......................	$324 00	
Knapp, F. D., attendant, 3 " 24 days	92 20	
Kuhn, C. A., " 1 month, 13 "	11 20	
Langan, C. A., " 12 months	324 00	
Long, G. F., " 11 " 28 days..........	358 00	
Langhoff, Aug., baker, 12 months	540 00	
Lawlers, J. T., kitchen, 3 " 14 days.......	58 93	
Laycock, Arthur, plumber, 23 days...................	23 00	
Lemmon, F. L., dining room, 4 days	2 13	
Love, James, night-watch, 12 months........................	420 00	
Layhe, Daniel, supervisor, 12 "	420 00	
Long, J. H., clerk, 1 month, ...	25 00	
Lagger, Wm., fireman, 6 months, 21 days..............	201 00	
Long, Elzy, laundry, 12 "	120 00	
Lyman, Clyde, attendant, 3 " 17 days	91 80	
Lavenberg, J. O., stenographer, 2 days..................	3 00	
Lannen, E. J., " 6 "	6 00	
Mandeville, A. F., attendant, 12 months	324 00	
McPhail, John, " 6 " 29 days...	209 00	
Martin, E. C., " 12 "	343 66	
McFarland, J. H., " 12 "	358 00	
Mowery, Peter, fireman, 11 " 25 days........	339 80	
Merillat, E., attendant, 12 "	324 00	
McKenzie, Duncan, florist, 12 "	480 00	
Mandeville, W. J., usher, 12 "	300 00	
McNamara, T. J., night phone, 1 month.......	15 00	
Morrow, George, attendant, 6 days	5 20	
Miller, C. S., Supt. G. and W. W., 7 months......................	238 34	
McFadden, Chas., dining room, 14 days.....................	7 47	
Mills, P. A., farm, 1 month, 11 days.......	34 16	
McEwen, Thos., kitchen, 10 days.....................	5 67	
McCray, Lewis, attendant, 1½ days......................	1 30	
Miller, Wm., " 5 months, 4 days......	128 44	
Morrissey, Jas., kitchen, 4 " 13 "	75 83	
Nussbaumer, Sol. express, 12 "	300 00	
Neiswander, Louis, gardener, 12 months	480 00	
Nichols, Harry, attendant, 9 "	225 00	
Oswalt, Chas., dining room, 8 " 24 days..............	222 80	
O'Hearn, M., " 3 " 8 "	52 27	
Osborn, S. M., attendant, 25 days	21 85	
Purdy, J. M., fireman, 12 months	360 00	
Pool, N. A., attendant, 2 " 12 days.......................	57 60	
Prior, M., " 24 days.......................	19 20	
Rockefeller, W. J., attendant, 12 months	324 00	
Roadarmel, McCurdy, " 12 "	360 00	
Ruddock, Thomas, " 12 "	396 00	
Reed, S. F., baker, 12 months.......	360 00	
Ragan, C. S., butcher, 10 months	300 00	
Rippinger, N. E., cook, 12 months	300 00	
" John, dining room, 12 months	300 00	
Rhodes, Alvin, fireman, 10 months........	300 00	
Rockwell, L. K., attendant, 8 days	6 93	
Riley, F. H., laundry, 12 months....	300 00	
Raab, F. J., operator, 12 "	420 00	
Reed, E. W., upholster, 12 months	480 00	
Riddle, Harry, kitchen, 2 " 8 days.......................	53 61	

CURRENT EXPENSES—Continued.

On what account.	Amount.	Total.
Wages—Male—Concluded.		
Roach, Chas., attendant, 16 days	$13 85	
Rawson, John, kitchen, 6 "	3 40	
Stadelman, Karl, attendant, 12 months	324 00	
Scott, Fred, " 6 " 2½ days	182 50	
Sphtgerber, R., laborer	23 77	
Spimuski, Alex., laborer	22 77	
Scott, C. O., attendant, 7 months	210 00	
" W. C., " 3 " 22 days	112 00	
Sackett, W. W., barn, 6 " 14 "	161 67	
Shuck, W. C., dining room, 11 months, 28 days	358 00	
Shepard, A. T., " 12 "	166 64	
Smith, Lynford, " 5 " 7 days	94 20	
Sandy, Festus, " 12 "	192 00	
Sharrock, S. H., night-watch, 12 months	384 00	
Sherman, A. W., " 12 "	384 00	
" W. H., " 12 " 17 days	347 00	
Snell, F. E., supervisor, 12 "	600 00	
Schunner, Eugene, dining room, 5 months, 27 days	94 39	
Spayd, Edw., attendant, 2 " 28 "	76 23	
Stegmeyer, H., dining room, 2 " 1 day	32 53	
Todd, F. A., " 11 "	183 31	
Taylor, C. A., labor, 12 "	120 00	
Turney, Milton, attendant, 6 " 16 days	174 77	
Tyler, Chas., barn, 1 month, 28 days	48 32	
Tillman, Frank, attendant, 9 "	7 79	
Vaughn, Harry, " 3 months, 1 day	88 60	
VanNatta, C. F., " 10 " 25 days	300 10	
" Bird, dining room, 5 months, 23 days	91 57	
VanMier, Samuel, attendant, 4 " 18 "	122 07	
Willard, C. W., " 12 "	324 00	
Westenhaver, C. R., kitchen, 12 "	208 00	
Walls, H. C., stenographer, 12 "	420 00	
Wise, Hugh, attendant, 3 " 22 days	97 98	
Zweiful, George, baker, 4 " 19 "	78 77	
Wages—Female.		$34,097 94
Bisling, Barbara, cook, 9 months, 16 days	$152 52	
Boelter, Alma, ironing room, 1 month, 19 days	19 60	
Bechtol, Mollie, attendant, 10 months, 5 "	173 67	
Carens, Kate, " 5 " 3 "	96 80	
" Rose, " 12 "	216 00	
Cottrill, Cora, " 12 "	218 00	
Christiansen, Fannie, attendant, 12 months	168 00	
Conley, Etta, cook, 12 months	192 00	
Cook, Iva, dining room, 12 months	216 00	
Cotter, Mame, " 12 "	168 00	
Cunningham, Margaret, laundry, 12 months	172 00	
Carpenter, Mae, marking room, 12 "	216 00	
Cool, Ella, attendant, 11 months, 5 days	206 00	
Copeland, Josephine, attendant, 8 months, 28 days	169 80	
Cotton, Dora, " 4 " 22 "	87 20	
Dry, Maggie, " 6 " 21 "	122 60	
Dimke, Augusta, dining room, 10 " 14 "	209 32	
Donnelly, M. A., ironing room, 6 "	77 00	
Daly, Lizzie, night-watch, 8 " 16 days	70 60	

CURRENT EXPENSES—Continued.

On what account.	Amount.	Total.

Wages—Female—Continued.

On what account.	Amount.	Total.
Doster, Emma, attendant, 9 months, 15 days	$172 50	
Emig, Maggie, dining room, 11 months, 23 days	164 72	
Eisenbeis, Anna, ironing room, 7 " 22 "	108 25	
" Rose, " 7 " 22 "	92 80	
Faber, Mary, attendant, 5 " 26 "	108 60	
Foote, Carrie, " 1 month, 16 "	27 60	
Fuller, Josephine, ironing room, 15 days	6 00	
Gilchrist, Alice, attendant, 12 months	216 60	
Guile, Effie, " 12 "	213 00	
Geogline, Amanda, attendant, 7 months	140 00	
Henderson, Lou, " 12 "	222 00	
Hoge, Florence, " 12 "	288 00	
Horn, Nanna, " 12 "	240 00	
Haly, Mary, cook, 12 months	192 00	
Hughes, Rose, laundry, 11 months	275 00	
Hartnett, Mary, " 12 "	184 00	
Hagerty, Anna, sewing room, 12 months	216 00	
Hughes, Mae, ironing room, 10 months, 7 days	130 80	
Hoge, Mary, " 2 " 4 "	25 60	
Harvey, Genoa, attendant, 2 " 12 "	43 20	
Inskeep, Minnie, " 7 " 16 "	135 60	
" Bertha, " 12 "	216 00	
Knapp, Anna, " 12 "	216 00	
Kelley, Juliette, supervisor, 12 "	336 00	
Knapp, Georgia, attendant, 5 " 5 days	94 73	
Leist, Kate, attendant, 7 months, 3 days	129 00	
Larkins, Anna, night-watch, 12 months	240 00	
Lupton, Dr. Ella G., physician, 4 months, 15 days	262 50	
Lemmon, Faye, attendant, 4 months, 6 days	72 20	
LaBeau, Elida, ironing room, 2 months, 13 days	29 20	
Miller, Emma, attendant, 11 months, 21 days	221 98	
McCue, Nellie, " 5 " 12 "	112 80	
Moran, Margaret, " 1 month, 21 "	32 30	
McKelvey, Lenore, " 12 months	238 00	
Monahan, Eva, chambermaid, 12 months	168 00	
Murbach, Lizzie, " 12 "	171 00	
Monahan, Minnie, cook, 12 months	244 93	
Mathews, Effie, attendant, 12 months	214 20	
Manner, Clara, laundry, 12 "	168 00	
Mowery, Etta, " 9 " 17 days	133 93	
Mutchler, Julia, attendant, 6 " 14 "	119 40	
Miller, Maude, dining room, 4 " 10 "	57 38	
Mathews, Fannie, ironing room, 4 months, 28 days	59 20	
Niles, Lizzie, attendant, 12 months	285 00	
Newell, Laura, " 6 " 3 days	102 60	
Owens, Irene, " 6 " 12 "	127 20	
" Ida, " 12 "	260 00	
O'Connor, Mary, " 12 "	211 00	
" M. G., " 9 " 17 days	180 06	
O'Connell, Kate, " 10 " 8 "	195 80	
Prichard, Jennie, " 11 " 16 "	230 66	
Perry, Hattie, cook, 4 months, 9 days	61 51	
Pedigo, Nora, ironing room, 2 months	24 00	
Purdy, Nora, laundry, 2 months, 1 day	28 46	
Probert, Anna, " 1 month	10 00	
Raab, Florence, attendant, 12 months	216 00	

CURRENT EXPENSES—Continued.

On what account.	Amount.	Total.
Wages—Female—Concluded.		
Rooke, Kate, attendant, 12 months	$236 33	
Ruh, Kayte, " 12 "	252 00	
Ruddock, Ferna, " 8 " 11 days...	185 05	
Robertson, Kate, " 8 " 13 "	155 20	
Rockefeller, Clara, " 12 "	300 00	
Riley, Mrs. F. H., assorting room, 11 months, 20 days..	210 00	
Roach, Lizzie, chambermaid, 11 months, 16 days.................	173 00	
Reilley, Kate, kitchen, 5 months, 22 days.......	114 82	
Ragan, Mrs. C. S., raising chickens, 12 months.............	59 50	
Smith, Lizzie, attendant, 12 months.......................	216 00	
Sherman, Gertrude, attendant, 12 months........	222 00	
Shaffer, Cora, attendant, 12 months	235 00	
Sherman, Grace, " 12 "	240 00	
Snell, Clara, assistant matron, 12 months	300 00	
Sullivan, Ella, chambermaid, 12 "	168 00	
Shuck, Lulu, dining room, 12 "	216 00	
Shields, Mary, attendant, 12 "	248 00	
Squires, Clara, " 7 days........	4 20	
Snyder, Mayme, ironing room, 3 months, 29 days	47 60	
Shafer, Mae, " 2 " 23 "	33 20	
Sherman, Leona, laundry, 1 month	12 00	
Taylor, Martha, attendant, 8 months, 18 days.........	163 80	
Turney, Mattie, " 26 days.....................	14 85	
" Lillian, ironing room, 1 month, 14 days	17 60	
Van Dusen, Clara, attendant, 2 months, 8 days..............	43 07	
Willard, Clara, " 6 " 14 "	116 40	
Wright, Ida, " 12 "	240 00	
Walton, Ida, " 5 " 8 days	113 33	
Warren, Ollie, " 11 " 26 "	237 32	
Wells, Julia, dining room, 12 "	192 00	
" Alice, ironing " 12 "	156 00	
Walsh, Bessie, laundry, 12 "	168 00	
Willard, Ines, attendant, 7 " 21 days	143 13	
Williams, Minerva, night-watch, 12 months	240 00	
Widner, Lida, supervisor, 12 months	300 00	
Williams, Hattie, attendant, 11 months, 28 days.................	209 80	
Wooley, Clara, " 7 " 15 " ....:...	132 00	
Zacharias, Tracy, " 12 "	240 00	
Zwicker, Mamie, " 18 days...............................	10 80	$17,987 38
Miscellaneous.		
Aprons, oiled, 36	$23 40	
Advance copies of report, 1,500 ....,....,..........	193 55	
Anthems, 14	11 25	
Birch seats, 72	2 52	
Byer, Jos P., services as secretary	28 56	
Boars, 2	19 00	
Cultivator, 1.................	24 00	
Clocks, 36	27 00	
Car tickets........................•••••	43 90	
Corn, 81,900................	42 63	
City Directory..	6 00	
Cutting hay and oats	45 28	
Dial ....,..	1 00	
Drill rental..•.••••••.......	5 10	

CURRENT EXPENSES—Concluded.

On what account.	Amount.	Total.
Miscellaneous—Concluded.		
Fire extinguisher	$8 00	
Filtering tubes, 3	3 00	
Ferrets, 2	5 00	
Flour sacks, 632	54 02	
Fertilizer, 4 tons	80 00	
Gas	1 57	
Horses, 2	240 00	
Horse care	8 25	
Hay rake	15 00	
Jointers, 2	4 25	
Livery hire	2 50	
Land rental	230 00	
Machine bands, ½ dozen	1 50	
Meat skewers, 1 M	35	
Medical journals	15 95	
Meals in city	75	
Metal polish, 200 pounds	32 00	
Manure, 8 loads	2 00	
Postoffice box rent	12 00	
Photo supplies	54 85	
Photos for report	300 00	
Razors honed	33 00	
Rental on typewriter	7 50	
Storage on baggage	45	
Spectacles repaired	25	
Stereopticon appliances	85 91	
Screenings, 23.500 pounds	19 16	
Sleeve, 1 6-inch	2 10	
Shovels, ½ dozen	1 32	
Silver polish, 4 dozen	6 00	
Slate, 200	8 00	
Shot, 235 pounds	8 81	
Threshing	24 20	
Tobacco dust	10	
Tools lost in sewer	7 75	
Toledo Critic, 300	45 00	
Tuning pianos	35 60	
Vials, 2	2 00	
Water purifier, 2,019 pounds	131 25	
Watch repaired	1 75	
Paris green, 100 pounds	18 50	
Pipe, 782 feet	9 46	$1,992 29
Total		$180,733 00

SALARIES OF OFFICERS AND SECRETARY AND EXPENSES OF TRUSTEES.

Name and occupation.	Amount.
Tobey, H. A., superintendent, 12 months	$1,200 00
Hamblin, R. E., steward, 5 months, 6 days..	346 65
Miller, C. S., steward, 6 months, 24 days.......................................	453 33
Todd, F. A., physician, 12 months ....`.`	700 00
Shepard, A. F., " 12 "	700 00
Cooper, W. G., " 12 "	700 00
Lupton, Ella G., " 7 "	408 33
Miller, C. S., storekeeper, 5 " 2 days...................	253 33
Garrett, E. M., " 6 " 28 days... .	346 67
Tobey, M. C., matron, 12 "	400 00
Foster, Charles, traveling expenses............	46 00
Campbell, G. P., "	16 00
Foster, Parks, "	60 00
Cole, L. C., "	18 00
Tobey, H. A., secretary of Board, 11 months	366 67
Total.....................	$6,009 98

ORDINARY REPAIRS, ETC.

Voucher.	To whom paid.	Amount.
81	Laborers' pay roll, wages	$234 33
82	Kopf, Fred, wagon repaired	33 20
83	Leibus & Cooper, asbestos backs	17 00
84	Neitzel, Wm., tools sharpened	1 49
85	Sattler, Peter, harness repaired	11 95
86	The Bostwick-Braun Co., hardware	72 72
87	National Supply Co., engineers' supplies............	21 94
88	S. B. & S. Vail Co., pump	350 00
89	Toledo Linseed Oil Co , oil	38 26
90	Wabash Railroad Co., gravel	115 50
91	Wolf, A. G., & Bros., ventilating machine..........	20 00
163	Laborers' pay roll, wages.................................	490 50
164	Appleton, D., & Co., subscription	5 00
165	Clow, Jas. B., & Sons, closets	37 85
166	Donovan Wire & Iron Works, guards	3 45
167	Hoffer, Fred, tank..	13 50
168	Kopf, Fred, wagon repaired...............................	51 80
169	Lansing Wheelbarrow Co., cart..........................	25 38
170	Neel, Henry, paints	18 06
171	Neukom, Albert, stone	6 50
172	Sterling & Co., upholsterers' supplies...............	41 67
173	Sattler, Peter, harness repairs	2 20
174	Tuley, Henry, A. M. D., subscription	4 00
175	The Brown, Eager & Hull Co., books..........'......	10 00
176	The Bissell, Dodge & Erner Co., electrical supplies	121 85
177	The Bostwick-Braun Co., hardware	83 96
178	The I. Journ. of Surg. Co., subscription	3 00
179	The Lion Dry Goods Co., carpets	150 75
180	The Morton Truck and Storage Co., drayage........	20 80
181	The M. I. Wilcox Co., asbestos	7 24
182	The Meilink Furniture Co., twine	2 00
183	The P. & T. Degnan Co., cement, etc	17 80
184	The Storrs & Harrison Co., shrubs.....................	18 20
185	The Vulcan Iron Works, plates	12 76
186	The Wilson Clark Co., water purifier	32 63
187	The Whitaker & Mitchell Hardware Co., hardware..	14 45
188	Welsbach Com. Co., lamps	16 15
259	Laborers' pay roll, wages	345 00
260	City of Toledo, pipes..	37 70
261	Foster Bros. Mfg. Co., beds	110 40
262	Kopf, Fred, wagon repairs	5 92
263	McClurg, A. H., & Co , books	41 73
264	Neel, Henry, paints	9 58
265	Newman, Dr. H. P., subscription	5 00
266	Peter, Wm., lumber	30 98
267	Sattler, Peter, harness repairs	4 80
268	The Bostwick-Braun Co., hardware	70 41
269	The Bissell, Dodge & Erner Co., electrical supplies	18 77
270	The M. I Wilcox Co., asbestos	14 75
271	The Meilink Furniture Co., cane	12 05
272	The P. & T. Degnan Co., brick	73 54
273	The Toledo Brick Co., brick.............................	16 00
274	The Toledo Supply Co., engineers' supplies........	24 51
275	Westerman, T., & Co , bread mixer......................	275 00
347	Laborers' pay roll, wages	294 31
348	Baker Bros., repairs on jig saw.........................	2 00
349	Bausch & Lamb Opt. Co., centrifuge	9 00
350	Crippen Bros., car pushers...............................	20 00

ORDINARY REPAIRS, ETC —Continued.

Voucher.	To whom paid.	Amount.
351	Eldridge, M. F., carriage repairs	$2 25
352	Fischer, Aaron, tees	3 84
853	Greene, J. W., & Co., machine repairs	8 33
354	Haynes, D. C., & Co., subscription	3 00
355	Jacobs, J , brick, etc	7 37
356	Lechtenbacher, L , broken stone	12 44
857	Lindon & Schumacher, floor tile	24 22
358	Peter, Wm., lumber	33 46
359	Parsh, Mason, traveling expenses	5 50
360	Sattler, Peter, harness repairs	2 60
361	The Bostwick-Braun Co., hardware	17 28
362	The Bissell, Dodge & Erner Co., electrical supplies	9 58
863	The Lion Dry Goods Co., carpets	214 13
364	The Meilink Furniture Co., furniture	16 00
365	The National Supp'y Co., engineers' supplies	158 78
366	The Rawson Electrical Co., phone repairs	1 50
867	The Shaw-Kendall Engine Co., engine, etc	179 05
368	The Tubular Axle Co., axle	3 50
869	The Toledo Rubber Co., hose	40 00
370	The Whitaker & Mitchell Hardware Co., hardware	14 48
442	Laborers' pay roll, wages	337 61
443	Buchholz, Gus, contract on duct	125 00
444	Bausch & Lamb Opt. Co., tubes	1 39
445	Bissell, F., & Co., electrical supplies	46 08
446	Culbertson, M. J., & Co., subscription	18 00
447	Cooney, M. J., & Co., carriage repairs	11 50
448	Eldridge, M. F., carriage repairs	2 50
449	Haynes, D. O., & Co., subscription	3 00
450	Lea Bros., & Co., subscription	8 75
451	McClurg, A. C., & Co., books	10 33
452	Peter, Wm , lumber	140 55
459	Ricard Boiler and Engine Works, boiler repairs	3 35
454	Rumsey, J D., tile	46 55
455	Stevens, B. A., table, etc	265 35
4 6	Sattler, Peter, harness repairs	5 70
457	The Bostwick-Braun Co., hardware	73 93
458	The Heavy Hardware Co., hardware	50
459	The John Hopkins' Press, subscription	10 00
460	The Lion Dry Goods Co., carpets	34 24
461	The M. I. Wilcox Co., ducking	5 00
462	The National Supply Co., engineers' supplies	7 68
463	The P. & T. Degnan Co., sand, etc	130 94
464	The Rawson Electrical Co., phone repairs	1 70
465	The Toledo Brick Supply Co., brick	142 50
466	The Toledo Bending Co., singletrees	4 00
468	The Welsbach Com. Co., lamp repairs	65
469	Warren Electric Mfg. Co., laundry repairs	219 85
547	Laborers' pay roll, wages	476 00
548	Armor Plate Plant Co., map	5 00
549	Arbuckle, Ryan & Co , engine	250 00
550	Baker Bros., steel	2 25
551	The Bostwick-Braun Co., hardware	126 14
552	Bissell, F., & Co., electric supplies	22 19
558	Charities Review, subscription	2 00
554	Greene, J. W., & Co., machine repairs	2 30
555	Hoffer, Fred, pipe	6 70
556	Kopf, Fred, wagon repairs	16 13
557	Lansing Wheelbarrow Co., carts, etc	89 75

ORDINARY REPAIRS, ETC.—Continued.

Voucher.	To whom paid.	Amount.
558	Milmine, H. B., & Co., covers	$3 00
559	Nicks, J. E. T., tongs	1 00
560	The National Supply Co., engineers' supplies	67 53
561	Neel, Henry, paints	109 05
562	Neitzel, Wm., tools sharpened	79
563	Peter, Wm., lumber	114 21
564	The P. & T. Degnan Co., lime and pipe	17 94
565	The Ricard Boiler Co., boiler repairs	22 00
566	The Shaw-Kendall Co., hangers	2 70
567	Stevens, B. A., knives, etc	2 40
568	Sattler, Peter, harness repairs	8 50
569	Schauss Bros., chairs	75 00
570	Sterling & Co., opaque	27 60
571	The Toledo Supply Co., engineers' supplies	326 29
572	The Toledo Brick Co., brick	11 00
573	The M. I. Wilcox Co., cup grease	2 00
645	Laborers' pay roll, wages	581 64
646	The National Supply Co., engineers' supplies	473 98
647	Neel, Henry, paint and glass	27 23
648	Neitzel, Wm., sharpened tools	79
649	Peter, Wm., lumber	35 40
650	Sattler, Peter, harness repairs	7 05
651	The Storrs & Harrison Co., trees and shrubs	36 03
652	Sterling & Co., opaque	13 80
653	Straight Line Engraving Co., valve bushings	49 50
654	The Toledo Brick Co., brick	31 00
655	The Toledo Supply Co., engineers' supplies	413 04
656	The M. I. Wilcox Co., carpet felt	15 93
657	Bissell, T., & Co., electrical supplies	10 06
658	The Bostwick-Braun Co., hardware	79 41
659	Clapp, C. D., & Co., gas burner	3 50
660	The P. & T. Degnan Co., sand and cement	262 75
662	Garfield, P. W., medical books	12 00
663	Kopf, Fred, carriage repairs	24 85
664	Libbie, Henry, stone flagging	8 14
665	Moore, C. H., repairing lawn mower	8 30
666	The Whitaker-Mitchel Hardware Co., hardware	4 45
667	The Lion Dry Goods Co., carpets	126 58
802	Laborers' pay roll, wages	631 59
803	Bissell, T, & Co., electrical supplies	41 22
804	Greene, J. W., & Co., machine repairs	2 00
805	Hoffer, Fred, stove pipe	6 20
806	Kopf, Fred, carriage repairs	5 80
807	Kind & Kuhlman, cement	24 19
808	The Lion Dry Goods Co., carpet	265 14
809	Lussky, Payne & Co., mattress tufts	4 50
810	Moore. C. H., repairing lawn mower	9 80
811	Neel, Henry, paint and oil	39 05
812	The National Supply Co., engineers' supplies	427 00
813	The National Supply Co., engineers' supplies	877 06
814	Stolberg & Parks, tow, etc	19 25
815	Sattler, Peter, harness repairs	4 50
816	The M. I Wilcox Co., hose, etc	105 75
904	Laborers' pay roll, wages	324 65
905	The Bostwick-Braun Co., hardware	113 91
906	Green, J. W., & Co., machine repairs	3 05
907	The Lion Dry Goods Co., carpets and curtains	72 17
908	Neel, Henry, glass and paint	24 02

ORDINARY REPAIRS, ETC.—Continued.

Voucher.	To whom paid.	Amount.
909	Sterling & Co., draperies	$5 59
910	Sattler, Peter, harness repairs	5 10
911	Stolberg & Parks, book case	28 78
912	Tubular Axle Co., axles	4 50
913	The Whitaker-Mitchel Hardware Co., hardware	4 20
914	The M. I. Wilcox Co., rope and twine	26 32
915	Keiper Bros., upholsterers' supplies	11 09
916	The Shaw-Kendall Co., pump springs	9 90
917	Stilwell, Bierce & Smith Vaile Co	6 30
918	The Toledo Supply Co., pump valves	33 70
919	Delany & Co., pump rental and supplies	407 00
920	Lussky, Payne & Co., curled hair	44 76
921	Shauss Mfg. Co., upholsterers' supplies	63 00
1017	Laborers' pay roll, wages	265 25
1018	The Bostwick-Braun Co., hardware	136 55
1019	Clapp, C. D., range	101 20
1020	Dolphin Paint Co., varnish	7 25
1021	Greene, J. W., & Co., machine repairs	2 85
1022	Hardy, Geo. E., wrenches	8 13
1023	Neel, Henry, paints	45 65
1024	Sattler, Peter, harness repairs	8 65
1025	Strellinger, C. A., grindstone and frame	17 25
1026	Stevens & Frederick, wagon repairs	20 70
1027	The Shaw-Kendall Co., crank shaft	25 00
1028	The Toledo Supply Co., engineers' supplies	11 63
1029	Sterling & Co., carpet, etc	144 70
1030	The M. I. Wilcox Co., sheathing, etc	50 35
1031	Murphey, Wasey & Co., chairs	16 95
1032	Birkmayer & Rodemick Bros., gas stove	4 50
1033	Kopf, Fred, carriage repairs	24 10
1034	Kieper Bros., rope fiber	4 81
1035	Lussky, Payne & Co., pantosote	22 50
1036	The Philip Carey Mfg. Co., pipe covering	329 25
1141	Laborers' pay roll, wages	311 50
1142	The Bostwick-Braun Co., hardware	31 14
1143	Cooney, M. J., & Co., carriage repairs	60 40
1144	The Buckeye Paint and Varnish Co., varnish	21 40
1145	Donovan Wire and Iron Works, angle iron	3 06
1146	Foster Bros. Mfg. Co., iron beds	216 00
1147	Hahn, Chas. F., block and tackle	15 00
1148	Kopf, Fred, wagon repairs	75 05
1149	Neitzel, Wm., sharpening tools	1 44
1150	Oberdorf, David, painting buggies	10 00
1151	Loos, Adam. door guards	30 00
1152	McConnell, J. D., mortising machine	65 00
1153	Neel, Henry, paint and oil	55 01
1154	Stevens, B. A., repairing cooler	2 00
1155	Specialty Carriage Co., covered wagon	236 25
1156	Sterling & Co., carpets and draperies	68 75
1157	Stolberg & Parks, cots	8 00
1158	Sattler, Peter, harness and repairs	39 55
1159	The Shaw-Kendall Co., engineers' supplies	149 63
1160	The Toledo Wire and Iron Works, steam baskets	60 00
1161	The Toledo Blade Co, advertising	30
1162	The Toledo Supply Co., engineers' supplies	45 26
1163	The Wayner Mfg. Co., door numbers	5 24
1164	Beckman, L., repairing instruments	2 60
1265	Laborers' pay roll, wages	679 07

ORDINARY REPAIRS, ETC.—Concluded.

Voucher.	To whom paid.	Amount.
1266	Allen & Parkhurst, wall paper and repairs	$49 30
1267	The Bostwick-Braun Co., hardware	126 35
1268	Kieper Bros., rope fiber	11 91
1269	Hofer, Fred, slate	59 40
1270	Kopf, Fred, blacksmithing	4 60
1271	Moore, C. H., lawn mower repairs	1 80
1272	Neel, Henry, paints and oil	33 25
1273	The Shaw-Kendall Co., engineers' supplies	32 59
1274	Sterling & Co., carpets	151 10
1275	Sattler, Peter, harness repairs	8 90
1276	The Toledo Work House, brick	6 50
1277	The Toledo Bridge Co., iron beams	26 25
1278	The Toledo Linseed Oil Co., oil	18 66
1279	The Toledo Rubber Co., chair tips	1 35
1280	The Toledo Supply Co., engineers' supplies	62 09
1281	The M. I. Wilcox Co., sheathing paper	12 10
	Total	$17,124 21

DISPOSAL OF SEWAGE.

Voucher.	To whom paid.	Amount.
92	Bisling, Joseph, labor	$35 00
93	The P. & T. Degnan Co., pipe, etc	108 09
189	Bisling, Joseph, labor	35 00
371	Buchholz, Aug., labor	37 19
	Total	$215 28

ELEVATOR FOR BOILER HOUSE.

Voucher.	To whom paid.	Amount.
668	Houghton, F. C., Foundry and Machine Co., elevator..................	$350 00
669	Hofer, Fred, cornice	8 00
670	The P. & T. Degnan Co., cement	22 76
671	The Toledo Brick and Supply Co., brick	46 00
672	The Toledo Supply Co., engineers' supplies...............................	73 24
	Total..........	$500 00

KITCHEN, ETC.

Voucher.	To whom paid.	Amount.
667½	The Roseville Brick and Tile Co., fire brick..	$168 00
816½	Valentine, John labor and material..	1,000 00
817	Jacobs, Jacob, labor	121 75
818	Mott, J. L., Iron Works, closets.....	15 07
819	Milmine, H. B., & Co., grate................	5 00
820	Neukom, Albert, stone flagging	7 00
821	Pray, J. L., & Son, crushed stone	27 80
822	The Western Mineral Wool Co., mineral wool...........................	82 80
922	Laborers' pay roll, wages...........................	315 00
923	The P. & T. Degnan Co., sand, cement and lime..	326 24
924	Loomis, L. W., tinware .... ~..	218 17
925	Pray, J. L., & Son, crushed stone..	33 62
926	Stevenson Co., repairing door...	55 00
927	The Toledo Bridge Co., iron beam	28 30
928	Valentine, John, final estimate	532 70
1050	Laborers' pay roll, wages	402 09
1051	The P. & T. Degnan Co., cement and pipe	310 55
1052	The Toledo Work House, brick	13 50
1053	The Vulcan Iron Works, castings.....	78 22
1054	McClaren & Sprague, lumber	201 77
1055	The National Supply Co., engineers' supplies	182 92
1165	Laborers' pay roll, wages...	156 85
1166	Reihnert & Co., iron sink	68 00
1167	The Vulcan Iron Works, castings...	14 20
	Total..........	$4,864 55

ADDITION TO LAUNDRY.

Voucher.	To whom paid.	Amount.
673	Laborers' pay roll, wages..	$368 55
674	Peter, Wm., lumber	94 11
675	"	222 84
676	"	146 33
677	"	88 69
678	Saylor, E. E., labor...	50 00
679	The Bostwick-Braun Co., hardware	138 42
680	" " "	30 23
681	Keasby & Mattison Co., pipe covering	66 15
682	The National Supply Co., engineers' supplies	37 21
683	" " "	24 42
684	The P. & T. Degnan Co., cement, etc	189 16
685	" " "	71 63
686	" " "	255 25
687	" " "	53 90
688	Warren Electric Mfg. Co., mangle, etc..............................	800 00
689	" " cylinder	95 00
690	The Shaw-Kendall Co., engineers' supplies.........................	114 27
691	The Toledo Supply Co., "	58 54
692	" " "	41 30
693	Valentine, John, contract price	2,519 00
694	Watkins, F. M., dampener..	35 00
	Total...	$5,500 00

Lightning Source UK Ltd.
Milton Keynes UK
UKHW021852121118
332198UK00006B/326/P